Teaching Swift's
Gulliver's Travels

Approaches to Teaching
World Literature

Joseph Gibaldi, series editor

For a complete listing of titles,
see the last pages of this book.

Approaches to Teaching Swift's

Gulliver's Travels

Edited by

Edward J. Rielly

Consultant Editor
Michael DePorte

The Modern Language Association of America
New York   1988

© 1988 by The Modern Language Association of America
All rights reserved
Printed in the United States of America

For information about obtaining permission to reprint material from
MLA book publications, send your request by mail (see address below),
e-mail (permissions@mla.org), or fax (212 533-0680).

Library of Congress Cataloging-in-Publication Data

Approaches to teaching Swift's Gulliver's travels /
edited by Edward J. Rielly.
p. cm. — (Approaches to teaching world literature ; 18)
Bibliography: p. Includes index.
ISBN 0-87352-511-6 ISBN 0-87352-512-4 (pbk.)
1. Swift, Jonathan, 1667-1745. Gulliver's travels. 2. Swift, Jonathan,
1667-1745—Study and teaching. I. Rielly, Edward J. II. Series.
PR3724.G8A66 1988
823'.5—dc19   88-13148
ISSN 1059-1133

Cover illustration of the paperback edition: C.E. Brock,
illustration for *Gulliver's Travels*, book 2, engraving, 1894.

Third printing 1997. Printed on recycled paper

Published by The Modern Language Association of America
10 Astor Place, New York, New York 10003-6981

CONTENTS

Preface to the Series vii

Preface to the Volume viii

PART ONE: MATERIALS
Edward J. Rielly

Classroom Editions 3

Required and Recommended Student Readings 5

Audiovisual Materials 7

The Instructor's Library

Introduction 9
Standard Editions and Reference Works 9
Background Works 10
Biographical and Critical Works 11

PART TWO: APPROACHES

Introduction 15

Approaches

Gulliver's Travels and Controversy
Richard H. Rodino 18

Using Student Responses to Teach *Gulliver's Travels*
Frederik N. Smith 25

Big Men and Little Men, Houyhnhnms and Yahoos:
Structural Parallels and Meaning in *Gulliver's Travels*
Peter J. Schakel 30

The Multiple Identities of Gulliver's "Reader"
Janet E. Aikins 37

Teaching *Gulliver's Travels*
John F. Sena 44

Introducing Swift's Satiric Themes and Techniques: *Gulliver's Travels*, Part 2, Chapter 7
Sidney Gottlieb 52

Teaching the Third Voyage
Michael DePorte 57

"In what ordure hast thou dipped thy pencil?": Problems in Teaching Part 4
Brian Corman 63

Sexuality and the Body
  Christopher Fox   69

Gulliver the Dreamer
  Dolores Palomo   75

Parody in *Gulliver's Travels*
  Roger D. Lund   81

Swift's Letters in Teaching Tone and Technique in *Gulliver's Travels*
  Charles Pullen   89

Gulliveriana: Ways of Reading *Gulliver's Travels*
  Jeanne K. Welcher   96

"Wild" and "Circumstantial" Inventions: Interdisciplinary
    Possibilities for Teaching *Gulliver's Travels*
  Melinda Alliker Rabb   102

Assignments

The Use of Dramatic Readings of *Gulliver's Travels* to
    Foster Discussion
  David J. Leigh   109

Gulliver and CAI: "A Project for improving . . . Knowl-
    edge by practical and mechanical Operations"
  R B Reaves   113

Gulliver's Travels in a Utopias-Dystopias Course
  Milton Voigt   117

A Survey of Writing Assignments on *Gulliver's Travels*
  Edward J. Rielly   121

Teaching *Gulliver's Travels* in Freshman Composition
  Robert Keith Miller   123

Writing a Satire: Or, Everyone His or Her Own Swift
  Douglas Murray   126

Participants in Survey of *Gulliver's Travels* Instructors   129

Works Cited   130

Index   145

PREFACE TO THE SERIES

In *The Art of Teaching* Gilbert Highet wrote, "Bad teaching wastes a great deal of effort, and spoils many lives which might have been full of energy and happiness." All too many teachers have failed in their work, Highet argued, simply "because they have not thought about it." We hope that the Approaches to Teaching World Literature series sponsored by the Modern Language Association's Committee on Teaching and Related Professional Activities, will not only improve the craft—as well as the art—of teaching but also encourage serious and continuing discussion of the aims and methods of teaching literature.

The principal objective of the series is to collect within each volume different points of view on teaching a specific literary work, a literary tradition, or a writer widely taught at the undergraduate level. The preparation of each volume begins with a wide-ranging survey of instructors, thus enabling us to include in the volume the philosophies and approaches, thoughts and methods of scores of experienced teachers. The result is a sourcebook of material, information, and ideas on teaching the subject of the volume to undergraduates.

The series is intended to serve nonspecialists as well as specialists, inexperienced as well as experienced teachers, graduate students who wish to learn effective ways of teaching as well as senior professors who wish to compare their own approaches with those of colleagues in other schools. Of course, no volume in the series can ever substitute for erudition, intelligence, creativity, and sensitivity in teaching. We hope merely that each book will point readers in useful directions; at most each will offer only a first step in the long journey to successful teaching.

Joseph Gibaldi
Series Editor

PREFACE TO THE VOLUME

A volume on Jonathan Swift's *Travels into Several Remote Nations of the World*, or, as it is commonly known, *Gulliver's Travels*, rightly belongs in the Modern Language Association's Approaches to Teaching World Literature series, for few other works of the imagination have aroused such sustained interest, enthusiasm, and controversy. For over 250 years, readers have praised, attacked, imitated, interpreted, relished, and taught the book, variously judging it the work of a misanthropist, children's fare, or one of the world's greatest satires.

Although critics today rarely label Swift a misanthrope or categorize *Gulliver's Travels* as a child's book, many beginning students still respond in these ways. Moreover, satire—and Swiftian satire in particular—is especially challenging to teach. Its comic veneer readily induces undemanding or inexperienced readers to ignore its serious core and intention. A work like *Gulliver's Travels* also requires the reader to distinguish between topical and universal satire. Finally, Swift's is a truly complex satire, often problematic to interpret and comprehend.

Teaching *Gulliver's Travels*, then, presents instructors with many real difficulties. Besides grappling with the Swift-as-misanthrope and *Gulliver's Travels*-as-children's-literature perceptions, teachers must decide on how to deal with, among other things, the enormous amount of background material synthesized in the work, the generic questions the book raises, its seeming lack of structural and thematic unity, the author's often ambivalent attitude toward his "hero" and the peoples and creatures (e.g., the Houyhnhnms) he encounters during his voyages, and, perhaps most important of all, the essence of Swift's satire.

The purpose of this volume is to help with these and other challenges involved in teaching the *Travels*, especially to undergraduates. We hope that it will provide all teachers, no matter how veteran and accomplished, with new insights into their own teaching. But the model reader for this book is the nonspecialist with little teaching experience who plans to teach *Gulliver's Travels*. Everyone involved in preparing this volume has tried to keep this reader in mind and to be as clear, practical, and direct as possible. We have attempted to limit specialized jargon and to keep theory subservient to practice.

As with other volumes in the series, this book has grown largely out of responses to questionnaires distributed to a wide range of college teachers. The responses supplied much of the information contained in the "Materials" portion of the book. In this first part, the reader will find data on the most commonly used classroom editions, on reading assignments, and on audiovisual materials. "The Instructor's Library" concludes part 1 with a consideration of reference, background, biographical, and critical works that respondents have recommended to other instructors, particularly to beginning teachers. Part 2 includes essays on specific approaches to teaching *Gulliver's Travels* and short descriptions of assignments. The book ends with an appendix of participants in the survey, a list of works cited, and an index.

Responses to the questionnaire show that *Gulliver's Travels* appears on syllabi in a variety of courses: Swift studies, specialized eighteenth-century courses (e.g., Swift and Defoe, Age of Pope), the eighteenth-century survey (sometimes including the Restoration), British-literature surveys (typically at the sophomore level), world-literature and "literary-masterpiece" surveys (usually lower-level), both freshman and advanced composition, and a medley of other literature courses (e.g., Satire, Literature of Travel, The Novel, Introduction to Narrative, Utopias and Dystopias, Science and Literature, Science Fiction, Literature of Fantasy). Such diversity offers profound tribute to the richness of Swift's book. It also suggested caution to those who prepared this volume, a caution reflected in the absence of course categories in the table of contents. We have not attempted to designate the essays in part 2 as belonging to specific types of courses. To do so, we believe, might pigeonhole both the essay and the reader and, in implying that instructors should read only those essays that "fit" their own courses, might create unwarranted barriers between reader and essay. Instead, the reader is invited to examine all the essays and select pieces, large and small, for future use. The essays are, on the whole, descriptive rather than prescriptive; the volume does not seek to convert instructors from one approach to another. We have, in fact, deliberately chosen to include opposing views on teaching *Gulliver's Travels*.

I wish to thank many people who helped in preparing this volume. Foremost among them is Michael DePorte, the consulting editor, whose indispensable help was always offered with sensitivity and generosity. I am also indebted to Joseph Gibaldi, the series editor, for his patience and guidance. My gratitude goes as well to all those teachers of the *Travels* who spent considerable time, through their responses to the questionnaire, supplying me with the basis for this volume. From among these respondents, I would single out those who agreed to contribute essays. I thank my wife, Jeanne, for her encouragement. Finally, I am grateful to my students and to Saint Joseph's College, North Windham, Maine.

EJR

Part One

MATERIALS

Edward J. Rielly

Classroom Editions

Choosing a classroom edition is one of the most important decisions that an instructor must make when planning a course. Instructors cite a number of factors involved in their decisions, including the quality of the introduction, the scope of explanatory and textual notes, the presence or absence of interpretive or background materials, the price of the edition, the publication date (especially when the instructor is evaluating whether the introduction, notes, or supplemental materials are up to date), and the reliability of the text itself.

Given the many variables involved, it is not surprising that no single edition satisfies everyone. In fact, one probably can say with reasonable accuracy that if an edition of *Gulliver's Travels* is in print (especially in paperback), someone is using it somewhere as a classroom text. Nonetheless, certain choices have proved particularly popular. The most commonly used text is the Norton Critical Edition, edited by Robert A. Greenberg, or its companion, the Norton *Writings of Jonathan Swift*, edited by Greenberg and William B. Piper. More than half the respondents report that they have used one of these editions in one or more courses in which they teach the *Travels*. Among reasons cited are the supplementary materials (e.g., Swift's correspondence, Pope's poetry on the *Travels*, and the critical essays by many leading Swift scholars of this century) and the text, based largely on the 1735 Faulkner edition. Instructors who use the *Writings* cite the presence of other selections by Swift (e.g., *A Tale of a Tub, The Battle of the Books, A Modest Proposal*) as a major reason for their choice. Some speak of the modest price, although the cost of the *Writings* is about twice that of the *Travels*. The chief attraction of the Norton Critical Editions, however, remains the presence of critical essays and other background material.

Not far behind the combined Norton Critical Editions is Louis Landa's Riverside Edition. Like Norton, Riverside offers the *Travels* in two editions, alone or with other selections. Unlike the Norton editions, the Riverside do not include critical essays or background materials. Many respondents who have used one of the Riverside editions praise Landa's introduction, which seems to parallel the Norton critical essays as a primary selling point, even though some note that it is a bit dated. Instructors also value Landa's notes and, when they use the Gulliver's Travels *and Other Writings* version, the additional Swift selections (e.g., *Tale of a Tub, Battle of the Books, Bickerstaff Papers*). Some seem emotionally attached to this Landa edition because they used it themselves as graduate students.

About an equal number of respondents (roughly a fifth) use either *The Norton Anthology of English Literature* (in the two-volume set or the one-volume *Major Authors Edition*) or Miriam Kosh Starkman's *Swift:* Gulliver's Travels *and Other Writings* (Bantam). Those who choose the *Norton Anthology* are usually teaching a lower-level survey and have chosen the *Anthology* for reasons other than its presentation of the *Travels*. In fact, many dislike the abridged version in the *Norton Anthology* (parts 1, 2, and 4, with only portions of part 3) but like the *Anthology* for other reasons or are obliged by departmental requirements to use it. The Bantam edition appeals primarily to those who are concerned about cost, although some instructors also find the introduction useful and the critical apparatus at least adequate.

Other less frequently used editions include the Modern Library College Edition of Gulliver's Travels *and Other Writings*, edited by Ricardo Quintana, and the Signet Classic *Gulliver's Travels*, with a foreword by Marcus Cunliffe. Price plays an important role in the selection of both these editions, and the typeface is a pleasing aspect of the Modern Library edition.

Certain editions, then, are clearly the most popular, but comments show that many instructors use more than one edition, tailoring their choice to the course, as well as to their own changing perceptions of the strengths and weaknesses of the various editions.

Required and Recommended Student Readings

Perhaps because *Gulliver's Travels* is organized in four parts, the book lends itself to abridgment. Most respondents, however, prefer to take all or nothing, arguing that a partial reading of the *Travels* yields only a partial appreciation. Few dispute this position, but some teachers of *Gulliver's Travels* are forced to work out a compromise because of time limitations, especially in survey courses. Others, principally those who use *The Norton Anthology of English Literature*, must make do with those portions of the book that are anthologized in their textbook. Instructors who question the importance of part 3, the section most often abridged or eliminated, should read Michael DePorte's essay in this volume.

In contrast to those who use an abridged version of part 3, a few instructors teach only that part—for example, in a course on the history of ideas or on a literature, science, and technology. Only part 4 is available for the few who teach the *Travels* in the Oxford *Restoration and the Eighteenth Century* anthology, edited by Martin Price, or in *The Norton Anthology of World Masterpieces*. It is possible, in fact, to find each of the four parts taught individually and to find any combination of two or more.

Instructors must also consider the merits of requiring supplemental readings, either critical or background, to accompany the *Travels*. In making this decision, they take into account such matters as type of course, specific objectives, level of students, quantity and difficulty of textbook readings, written assignments, and pedagogical methods. As one might expect, teachers in sophomore surveys or other introductory courses rarely supplement *Gulliver's Travels* with assigned readings, in part because the book (or a portion of it) is only a small segment of the course. Some instructors believe that students in introductory courses have enough work simply in doing the basic readings. Others are concerned that students may take refuge in secondary materials instead of developing their critical abilities.

These last two concerns also figure prominently in planning of upper-level courses, including Restoration and eighteenth-century surveys. More than half the respondents do not require their students to read background or critical material.

Many instructors recommend and some require extra readings, usually by distributing bibliographies and/or placing works on reserve in their libraries. The most popular source of supplemental readings is one of the Norton Critical Editions, when that book serves as a classroom text. Among the most commonly assigned readings from

Norton are R. S. Crane's "The Rationale of the Fourth Voyage" and "The Houyhnhnms, the Yahoos, and the History of Ideas" and Samuel Holt Monk's "The Pride of Lemuel Gulliver." For biographical background, several instructors assign selections from Irvin Ehrenpreis's three-volume *Swift: The Man, His Works, and the Age.*

A popular introductory volume (usually in courses focusing on Swift) is Ricardo Quintana's *Swift: An Introduction.* When assigning supplemental readings from Swift himself, instructors usually choose from among *A Modest Proposal, The Battle of the Books, The Mechanical Operation of the Spirit,* a selection of his poems, and part or all of *A Tale of a Tub.* These selections serve to highlight and clarify themes, satiric objects, and satiric methods in *Gulliver's Travels.* The contemporary work most often read in conjunction with the *Travels* is Defoe's *Robinson Crusoe,* which usually stands in the curriculum as an equal to the *Travels,* unlike such "illustrative" assignments as portions of the *Philosophical Transactions of the Royal Society* or selections from Dampier's accounts of his voyages. Another contemporary work taught with the *Travels* is Montesquieu's *Les lettres persanes,* as an interesting contrast to Swift's book: exotic foreigners in a familiar land as opposed to the familiar Gulliver in exotic lands. Beyond these selections, many other related works are assigned or, more commonly, recommended (e.g., Voltaire's *Candide*). Consult "The Instructor's Library" below for additional titles appropriate to advanced students as well as to teachers of the *Travels.*

Audiovisual Materials

A majority of the respondents to the *Gulliver's Travels* questionnaire do not use audiovisual aids. Those who do, however, utilize an interesting range of materials. Most common are reproductions of illustrations from editions of the *Travels*; of particular use here is the Isaac Asimov edition, *The Annotated* Gulliver's Travels. The following incorporates most of the audiovisual aids that respondents mention: illustrations from works contemporary with or preceding Swift, printo from the period, maps (both real and fictional), Gulliveriana (poems, continuations, parodies, etc.), filmstrips (most mentioning Swift only briefly), film versions of the *Travels*, children's versions, recording of Georg Telemann's *Gulliver-Suite*, "The Majestic Clockwork" in the *Ascent of Man* television series, recorded readings from Swift's works, recorded discussions of Swift's works.

Most instructors who employ audiovisual aids make limited but significant use of them for various purposes of enrichment. A few, however, incorporate these materials into the heart of their teaching; in this volume, Melinda Alliker Rabb, John F. Sena, and Jeanne K. Welcher describe their handling of illustrations, Telemann's *Gulliver-Suite*, selected Gulliveriana, and other aids. Teachers interested in expanding their own use of audiovisual materials should read these three essays for both methods and sources and should consult catalogs of available films, filmstrips, and audiocassettes. Gould Media (44 Parkway West, Mount Vernon, NY 10552) for example, offers at least five audiocassettes of scholars discussing Swift and his writings, among them Angus Ross on the *Travels* and Mary Elizabeth Bowen on Swift and scientific satire. Michael Redgrave reads episodes from the *Travels* on a cassette available from Listening Library, Inc. (1 Park Ave., Old Greenwich, CT 06870).

No outstanding film version of the *Travels* exists, but instructors might wish to use the partially animated 1977 version of the voyage to Lilliput, starring Richard Harris. This film can be ordered from Guidance Associates (Communications Park, Box 3000, Mount Kisco, NY 10549). A 1939 animated feature version of *Gulliver's Travels* is distributed by Audio-Brandon Films (34 MacQuesten Parkway South, Mount Vernon, NY 10550) but is also widely available in video-rental stores. A current filmstrip series that gives some attention to Swift is *The Age of Reason* (Films for the Humanities, Box 2053, Princeton, NJ 08543). This selective list of companies is intended not as an endorsement of their products but as a reminder that audiovisual aids are reasonably easy to acquire, through either purchase or rental.

Catalogs and interlibrary-loan programs make audiovisual aids accessible to everyone.

Of related value are dramatic readings and performances by students within the classroom. As David Leigh's essay makes clear, performance techniques can also have a place in teaching *Gulliver's Travels*.

The Instructor's Library

Introduction

Experienced Swift scholars and teachers will be familiar with most of the books and articles cited in this section of the volume. Beginning teachers, generalists, and specialists in other areas, however, may find much here to help them. The guiding principle behind the preparation of this section is the desire to assist an instructor who is teaching Swift for the first time or whose formal training has been primarily in other areas. Thus, we have made no attempt to include every book or article that might somehow be helpful, or even every work mentioned on the questionnaires. Nor have we included works with which a college instructor is normally familiar, like *The Cambridge Bibliography of English Literature*.

Standard Editions and Reference Works

A teacher of *Gulliver's Travels* should be familiar with the standard edition of Swift's prose, *The Prose Works of Jonathan Swift*, edited by Herbert J. Davis et al., even though the instructor will not use this edition as a classroom text. Originally in fourteen volumes, the edition now includes the two-volume edition of *The Journal to Stella*, edited by Harold Williams (initially published separately). Of particular importance, of course, is volume 11, the *Travels*; the new teacher should consult at least its introduction. Harold Williams has also edited the poetry and letters—*The Poems of Jonathan Swift* (3 vols.) and *The Correspondence of Jonathan Swift* (5 vols.)—as well as *Gulliver's Travels: The Text of the First Edition*, which might be useful, particularly the introduction and notes, on the writing, publishing, and revising of the *Travels*. The instructor who wants a handy one-volume edition of selections from Swift might acquire a copy of the recently published *Jonathan Swift* volume in the Oxford Authors series. This paperback, edited by Angus Ross and David Woolley, contains a rich selection of Swift's writings (excluding the *Travels*), useful notes, a fine bibliography, and a few extras, such as a chronology of Swift's life, a glossary of terms, and a biographical index of contemporaries, with succinct identifications of persons mentioned in Swift's writings.

The beginning instructor also should know about several bibliographies of studies on Swift. These vary in years covered and inclusiveness, but taken together they are invaluable: L. A. Landa and J. E. Tobin, *Jonathan Swift: A List of Critical Studies Published from 1895* to 1945; J. J. Stathis, *A Bibliography of Swift Studies, 1945-1965*; R. H. Rodino, *Swift Studies, 1965-1980: An Annotated Bibliography*; D. M. Vieth, *Swift's Poetry, 1900-1980: An Annotated Bibliography*. A bibliography of Swift's own writings is H. Teerink's *Bibliography of the Writings of Jonathan Swift*. Milton Voigt's review of modern scholarship in *Swift and the Twentieth Century* is also important.

Background Works

A wide range of background works is available for beginning teachers. The most popular book for general background is Donald Greene's *The Age of Exuberance: Backgrounds to Eighteenth-Century English Literature*. Greene's book includes sections entitled "The Country and Its People," "A Historical Summary," "Ideas and Attitudes," and "The Arts." With these summaries, the book offers useful chronologies.

For historical background, two readily obtainable paperbacks are Maurice Ashley's *England in the Seventeenth Century* and J. H. Plumb's *England in the Eighteenth Century*, both in the Pelican History of England series. While emphasizing political and military actions, the authors also consider the social and intellectual movements of their respective centuries. Another useful Pelican history is J. P. Kenyon's *Stuart England*. For a more political focus, there are Geoffrey Holmes's *British Politics in the Age of Anne*, Isaac Kramnick's *Bolingbroke and His Circle: The Politics of Nostalgia in the Age of Walpole*, and Bertrand Goldgar's *Walpole and the Wits: The Relation of Politics to Literature*. Useful for the social setting are Roy Porter's *English Society in the Eighteenth Century* and Dorothy George's *London Life in the Eighteenth Century*. Irish background is provided in J. C. Beckett's essay "Swift and the Anglo-Irish Tradition" and Oliver Ferguson's *Jonathan Swift and Ireland*.

An obvious work for scientific background is R. F. Jones's *Ancients and Moderns*. The scope of Jones's work is indicated by the subtitle, *A Study of the Rise of the Scientific Movement in Seventeenth-Century England*. Marjorie Nicolson's *Science and Imagination* includes two essential essays, "Swift's 'Flying Island' in the *Voyage to Laputa*" and "The Scientific Background of Swift's *Voyage to Laputa*," the second coauthored with Nora Mohler.

A number of works depicting other aspects of the intellectual background receive high praise. Basil Willey's *The Eighteenth Century Background* focuses on Swift in the chapter entitled " 'Nature' in Satire"; it also presents several other topics, including reason and natural morality, that would be helpful for the beginning instructor. Paul Fussell's *The Rhetorical World of Augustan Humanism* examines the humanistic view of humankind, as well as images and motifs that reflect this set of ethical conceptions. In *The Great Chain of Being*, Arthur Lovejoy examines the worldview expressed by the metaphor that furnishes his title. Phillip Harth's *Swift and Anglican Rationalism* is useful for the religious background, although he emphasizes Swift's *Tale of a Tub* more than the *Travels*. Louis Landa's *Swift and the Church of Ireland* is more explicitly historical. Aline M. Taylor's "Sights and Monsters and Gulliver's Voyage to Brobdingnag" is useful as background to part 2, in which the diminutive Gulliver is exhibited as a freak. Recommended for part 4 of the *Travels* is R. S. Crane's essay "The Houyhnhnms, the Yahoos, and the History of Ideas." Finally, contemporary texts are available: Clive Probyn's *Jonathan Swift: The Contemporary Background* contains twenty-three selections by writers of the late seventeenth and early eighteenth centuries.

Biographical and Critical Works

Every teacher of *Gulliver's Travels* should be acquainted with Irvin Ehrenpreis's majestic three-volume study of Swift's life, *Swift: The Man, His Works, and the Age*. Ricardo Quintana's *Swift: An Introduction* is also highly respected. As Quintana's subtitle implies, this book is a natural choice for an instructor new to the world of Swift. Quintana's earlier *Mind and Art of Jonathan Swift* is almost as popular with teachers of the *Travels*. To some, this volume is an even more effective introduction to Swift than is the *Introduction*. Kathleen Williams's excellent study of Swift's writings, *Jonathan Swift and the Age of Compromise*, is still valuable. David Nokes's recent *Jonathan Swift, a Hypocrite Reversed: A Critical Biography* offers some new directions in its evaluations of Swift.

Edward Rosenheim's *Swift and the Satirist's Art*, John Bullitt's *Jonathan Swift and the Anatomy of Satire*, and W. B. Carnochan's *Lemuel Gulliver's Mirror for Man* provide analyses of Swift's satiric techniques. F. P. Lock offers politicial explication in his *Politics of Gulliver's Travels*, and Phillip Harth's essay "The Problem of Political Allegory in *Gulliver's Travels*" is a useful short introduction to the political allegory.

Ehrenpreis's *The Personality of Jonathan Swift*, a collection of biographical and critical essays, remains useful despite his larger and more recent *Swift*. Arthur E. Case's *Four Essays on* Gulliver's Travels clarifies such matters as chronology, geography, and personal references in the *Travels*. C. J. Rawson's *Gulliver and the Gentle Reader: Studies in Swift and Our Time* is a highly praised and much more recent work. For eighteenth- and nineteenth-century responses to

Swift's book, consult *Swift: The Critical Heritage*, edited by Kathleen Williams.

A few articles have also been suggested: Samuel Holt Monk's "The Pride of Lemuel Gulliver," R. S. Crane's "The Houyhnhnms, the Yahoos, and the History of Ideas" (these first two mentioned earlier as popular required readings), Norman Brown's "The Excremental Vision" (valued as a stimulant to discussion), Roland Frye's "Swift's Yahoo and the Christian Symbols for Sin," and John Traugott's "A Voyage to Nowhere with Thomas More and Jonathan Swift: *Utopia* and *The Voyage to the Houyhnhnms*." James Clifford's formulation of interpretive categories in "Gulliver's Fourth Voyage: 'Hard' and 'Soft' Schools of Interpretation" is essential for a study of part 4 of the *Travels*. Another of Clifford's essays, "Argument and Understanding: Teaching through Controversy," offers an interesting pedagogical approach. Richard Rodino's essay in this volume suggests ways to apply this approach to the *Travels*.

Finally, a beginning teacher should note that many helpful articles, including some of those mentioned above, have been collected in such volumes as Ernest Tuveson's *Swift: A Collection of Critical Essays*, Frank Brady's *Twentieth Century Interpretations of* Gulliver's Travels: *A Collection of Critical Essays* (both of these readily available respectively in the Prentice-Hall Twentieth Century Views and Twentieth Century Interpretations series), A. N. Jeffares's *Fair Liberty Was All His Cry: A Tercentenary Tribute to Jonathan Swift*, Clive Probyn's *The Art of Jonathan Swift*, C. J. Rawson's *Focus: Swift* (and its new version, *The Character of Swift's Satire*), and John Traugott's *Discussions of Jonathan Swift*. Milton Foster's *A Casebook on Gulliver among the Houyhnhnms* includes both the text of part 4 and a wide range of interpretations of the final voyage (in both articles and excerpts from books). Unfortunately, the volume was published in 1961, so the selection is dated.

As many instructors note, the works they recommend to beginning teachers are equally useful to students. Instructors may wish to draw from the above discussion a list of appropriate required or recommended readings for their students. At the same time, the list could serve as the basis for library orders to fill in gaps on the shelves devoted to Jonathan Swift.

Part Two

APPROACHES

INTRODUCTION

Students of literature learn to approach a satirist carefully for fear of committing the kind of folly the satirist would have ridiculed. I have been particularly aware of this possibility while preparing this volume. What, one wonders, might Swift have made of our questionnaire? Would the "methods" proposed in the following essays sound too much like "systems" or "projects"? Might we suddenly find ourselves transported from our respective colleges and universities to the Academy of Lagado?

In the final analysis, I think not. Swift himself, after all, embarked on many projects and was especially interested in education—and very critical of miseducation. In the ninth *Intelligencer*, for example, he protests that "the very Maxims set up to direct *modern* Education, are enough to destroy all the Seeds of Knowledge, Honour, Wisdom and Virtue among us." Swift laments the current opinion "that the Study of *Greek* and *Latin* is Loss of Time; that the publick Schools by mingling the Sons of Noblemen with those of the Vulgar, engage the former in bad Company; . . . that to dance, fence, speak *French*, and know how to behave your self among great Persons of both Sexes, comprehends *the whole Duty of a Gentleman*" (*Prose Works*, Davis ed. 12: 48-49).

In the same paper, Swift exposes the ignorance of a military man engaged in a coffee-house diatribe against book learning:

> D—n me, Doctor, say what you will, the Army is the only School for Gentlemen. Do you think my Lord Marlborough beat the French with Greek and Latin. . . . D—n me, I would be glad, by G–d, to see any of your Scholars with his Nouns, and his Verbs, and his Philosophy, and Trigonometry, what a Figure he would make at a Siege or Blockade, or reconoitring. . . . (49)

The army veteran, as well as contemporary opinion, may have placed little value on sound humanistic learning, but Swift clearly did.

The essays that follow share Swift's commitment to excellence in education, as they explore a wide range of topics and instructional methods important to teachers of the *Travels*. The first two reflect several current trends in teaching *Gulliver's Travels*, particularly the popularity of reader-response criticism and the major influence of two essays by James L. Clifford: "Argument and Understanding: Teaching through Controversy" and "Gulliver's Fourth Voyage: 'Hard' and 'Soft' Schools of Interpretation." Richard H. Rodino builds on Clifford's concepts in his account of teaching through controversy, and Frederik N. Smith considers additional ways to use student responses.

Peter J. Schakel then relates his teaching of parallels in structure and meaning among parts 1, 2, and 4 of the *Travels*; Janet E. Aikins describes introducing students to Gulliver's implied readers; and John F. Sena narrates his class-by-class teaching of Swift's book. John Sena's essay, which surveys such specifics as the nature of satire, genre identification, writing assignments, discussion topics, and audiovisual materials, leads to the more localized essays that follow.

Each of the next six essays deals with an issue often cited by teachers as a particular problem, a matter of high priority, or both. Sidney Gottlieb presents his method of introducing students to Swift's satiric themes and techniques; Michael DePorte describes his teaching of the third voyage (and the voyage's relation to the rest of the *Travels*); and Brian Corman offers an overview of special problems relating to part 4, with an examination of common but unsatisfactory student responses. After Christopher Fox addresses his handling of sexuality in *Gulliver's Travels*, Dolores Palomo and Roger D. Lund turn to the subject of genre. Many teachers raise this topic, sometimes making it part of their teaching through controversy (for example, with the question "Is *Gulliver's Travels* a novel?"). But most ultimately move beyond the issue, believing that a discussion of genre can elicit insights about the book but should not become an end in itself. Dolores Palomo, without limiting the work by labeling it a novel, acknowledges its novelistic qualities; in the classroom, she presents Gulliver as a fictional character in order further to humanize the story. Roger Lund's approach is to teach the *Travels* as a parody of many types of literature, including the novel.

Many teachers of the *Travels* are adept at combining the old with the new. While assimilating recent understandings of educational psychology into their teaching, they also take their students back to Swift's own time. Charles Pullen uses Swift's letters in conjunction with the *Travels*, an approach that also helps his students master the intricacies of Swift's satiric tone and techniques. Jeanne K. Welcher details her use of Gulliveriana, including imitations, continuations, cartoons, and abridgments; and Melinda Alliker Rabb outlines her classroom work with illustrations from books contemporary with or antedating *Gulliver's Travels*. Both approaches bring audiovisuals into the center of the learning process. A majority of respondents to the questionnaire stated that they use no audiovisuals at all. After reading these two essays (and John Sena's), many are sure to reconsider.

The essays conclude with several discussions of assignments. David J. Leigh describes his use of dramatic readings; R. B. Reaves suggests developing computer-generated insights from question-and-answer sequences; and Milton Voigt tells how he teaches the *Travels* within a utopian-dystopian context. Other reading assignments are detailed in the "Required Readings" and "Instructor's Library" sections of part 1. Teachers also use a rich variety of writing projects in teaching the *Travels*. A survey of these assignments precedes Robert Keith Miller's account of using the *Travels* to generate writing topics and strategies in freshman English. The final essay, by Douglas Murray, discusses having students write satires of their own, often using techniques borrowed from *Gulliver's Travels*.

These essays address many but obviously not all pedagogical questions concerning *Gulliver's Travels*. They do not offer a definitive blueprint for teaching Swift's book. Devising teaching strategies is a proper function of the individual teacher, but we hope that these essays will assist teachers in carrying out this role, perhaps more by raising questions than by supplying answers. If the essays encourage us to question, reconsider, and analyze, they will help us become more effective teachers of the *Travels*—and they will have proved faithful to the spirit of Swift's masterpiece.

EJR

APPROACHES

Gulliver's Travels and Controversy
Richard H. Rodino

Screaming or grinning at critical quarrels over *Gulliver's Travels* has occupied interested readers for nearly three hundred years, illustrating at some level that Swift's chief end really was to "vex the world rather then divert it." Most ink has been spilt on book 4 in vain attempts to dissolve its interpretive opacity, to uncover the superiority of one interpretation to all competitors. Fortunately, a steady trickle of first-rate commentary, including that of George Sherburn, Wayne C. Booth, and James L. Clifford, has focused on the disagreements themselves, found considerable importance in them, and thereby clarified not only what *Gulliver's Travels* means but also the peculiar ways it expresses its meaning, exposing as a consequence some of the ways and means of literary criticism. The same double insight can be made available to undergraduates who have a little background in English studies, if we initiate them into these interpretive controversies.

The idea, simply put, is to assign to various students essays espousing conflicting interpretations of *Gulliver's Travels*, asking each student to represent the author's position in class as convincingly as possible, as a way of generating further discussion. Advocating this kind of teaching through controversy, the late James L. Clifford cautioned that it might on first sight appear daring. Are undergraduates sufficiently informed about Swift, or about the eighteenth century, or even about literary interpretation, to profit from grappling with a critical crux? Clifford's answer was emphatically positive: "the most successful way to stir up genuine interest is to move into areas where there have been major disagreements. Human beings being what we are, it is curiosity and doubt which stir up the most personal engagement" ("Argument and Understanding" 2).

A principal reward is that the students begin to inform one another, improving their lecture-class roles from listeners and note takers to active researchers, presenters, and defenders of a thesis, and, in discussion classes, freshening their dialogue in the current production of "what do *you* think about this passage?"

A second advantage is the way students' contexts may be broadened. For my modestly sophisticated undergraduate classes—primarily junior and senior English majors—teaching through controversy actually lightens the job of presenting background material on the author, the period, and the genre. The writing on *Gulliver's Travels*, while wonderfully disputatious, is also rich and scholarly. Selected with care, five or six essays or book chapters will introduce students to an impressive range of literary, biographical, historical, and even methodological contexts. For example, on the key question of whether the Houyhnhnms represent a genuine ideal, essays may be assigned that answer in terms of eighteenth-century economics (Landa, "Dismal Science"; Thorpe; Wilding). Other possibilities: attitudes toward Ireland (Kelly, Torchiana); religion (Ehrenpreis, "Origins"; Quintana, "Satiric Intent"; Landa, *Swift and the Church*; Kallich; McManmon; Radner); Swift's biography (Quintana, *Swift*; Ehrenpreis, *Swift*; Pierre); the "goût chinois" (Takase); theriophily and definitions of humanity (Gill, "Beast over Man"; Halewood and Levich; Wedel; Novak; Probyn, "Man, Horse and Drill"); comparative utopias in Plato (Crane, "Houyhnhnms"; Beauchamp; Reichert), Thomas More (Traugott, "Voyage"; Brink; Vickers), or Plutarch (Halewood); satiric traditions (Yeomans; Quintana, "Situational Satire"; Greene, "Education"); ideas about reason (Leigh, Douglas H. White, John H. White) or language (Castle; Philmus, "Language"); or any of numerous other contexts. As individual students expound some of these contexts, inevitably either supporting or questioning background materials already on the table, the whole class will be learning not only a great deal about Swift and the eighteenth century but also what literary scholars are interested in, what kinds of questions they ask, how they weigh the importance of different perspectives and contradictory information.

Does this approach seem apt to replace literature with criticism as the primary object of attention? My students certainly have never thought so. In fact, they thumb back through *Gulliver's Travels* more than they do most texts, as new glints on the debate send them searching for evidence to impugn someone else's point or to aid and abet their own. I have shared Clifford's experience of students who "rush off to do additional research to support their own position, or to clear up some mystery" ("Argument and Understanding" 2).

To be honest, as a postformalist critic I am not unhappy when my students begin to recognize an interdependency between text and interpretation—indeed, for me this is a third main benefit of teaching through controversy. Even a not-quite-committed poststructuralist may find the *Gulliver's Travels* controversy a most propitious opportunity for jarring 1980s students out of their nonresistance to received tropes of wisdom. Once they have seen certainty met with countercertainty, definitive answer with alternative answer, students of controversy may begin to confront a second order of literary knowledge: that at various times in history and culture critics notice features of *Gulliver's Travels* that were previously invisible; that both historical and formalistic methods, plus any combination of the two, are permanently entangled in a shifting network of culture, psychology, ideology, and rhetoric that permits them to discover certain meanings and to overlook or devalue still others; that preferring one literary interpretation to another has consequences. In Clifford's words, "[t]he value of this kind of approach is that it does make clear to every student just what the basic issues are, and what is involved in any personal choice of allegiance" ("Argument and Understanding" 3).

Students caught up in a controversy over Gulliver, his Houyhnhnms, and his Yahoos, are likely to insist that other students reassess their own (often unacknowledged) assumptions about how the heart is wiser than the head (or even about the duality of the two), about the purposelessness of cynicism, the specialness of human nature, the unavoidableness of religious consolation, the relationship of author to narrator and to characters, the functions of fictional characters, and much more. In an eighteenth-century-novel course, a teacher wishing to help this reevaluation along may guide the key disagreement about Gulliver as fictional character (satiric device or psychologically evolving character?) toward general insights into the novel and satire. In a period-survey course, the disagreements about which tradition of defining humankind is reflected in Houyhnhnm and Yahoo may felicitously prepare for a reading of *An Essay on Man*. At the very least, the controversy should serve to complicate the perennial undergraduate misconception that ideas in past eras were not bewilderingly numerous and diverse, as they are today, or that textbook nuggets are adequate adult guides to what a work of literary art means, let alone to what an entire historical period was able to think.

Introducing and shaping study of the first three voyages through the controversy over book 4 is hardly a strained idea, since Gulliver himself raises the issues of book 4, before the other voyages even begin, in his prefatory "Letter to Sympson." The four voyages are now generally granted a coherent design, although this was formerly a vexed issue. Both sides of the book 4 controversy chart overall thematic developments, although to quite different conclusions. Assuming that the first three books prepare for the voyage to Houyhnhnmland and are completed by it allows a class to study the political satire, the satire on pride, delusion, and hollow science, and the comparative utopias presented in the three books, with a keener sense of what is developing and what is at stake. One school of interpretation has additionally stressed the narrative's psychological consistency: Gulliver evolves as a character responding to stresses placed on him by his environment. Undergraduates may reread a little more shrewdly if they know what to search for: evidence of Gulliver's psychological debilitation, challenged by episodes that appear to undermine such coherent characterization—for example, the farcically inconsistent or fractiously satirical episodes, such as Gulliver's apparently plausible vindication of the sexual honor of a six-inch-tall lady (book 1, ch. 6). They can see that the payoff is large; predominant evidence of Gulliver's psychological deterioration might argue that his failures, not the Houyhnhnms', occupy the ironic foreground of book 4.

Before discussion officially begins on book 4, each student is assigned one substantial critical essay or book chapter. If the class is small enough, say twelve or fifteen, it may be advantageous to assign a separate article to each. In the classes of thirty to thirty-five we get at Holy Cross, I divide between five and eight essays evenly among them. Each student must prepare a good précis of the essay's argument and come to class ready to represent the author's position as convincingly as possible. When the class is small, each student may speak for a few minutes as the author's advocate; in a large group, one student may be asked to speak on behalf of each author.

A good way to introduce the controversy is through Clifford's analysis of the main categories of disagreement on book four ("'Hard' and 'Soft' Schools of Interpretation"), by means of either lecture or required reserve reading, or, for me best of all, by asking a student to present the argument of the essay to the class. Clifford's enjoyable essay begins with a brief history of earlier critical opinions, useful for establishing the vehemence of the Victorian response and the identification of character and author that fueled it. (The studies of Voigt, Clubb, or Shamsuddoha, or the anthologies edited by Brady, Foster, Gravil, Donoghue, or Williams, may also be used for this purpose.) Clifford goes on to categorize the main controversies over book 4: (1) the meaning of the Yahoos, (2) the meaning of the Houyhnhnms, (3) the significance of Pedro de Mendez, (4) the interpretation of the ending: Gulliver's final return to England as comic, satiric, shocking, tragic, or didactic.

From these interpretive coordinates, it is possible to chart two main opposing camps, the famous "hard" and "soft" schools. Neither side still sees the Yahoos as a crazy slander on human nature; most current hard- and soft-school readings alike now accept them as the theoretical limits to which human beings might degenerate. The Houyhnhnms, on the other hand, remain a vexed question, seen by soft-school critics as merely rational and certainly not ideal ("Would *you* want to live in a world with no emotions?"); or as cold, repulsive beings, lacking Christian benevolence; or else as mere images of prelapsarian perfection, irrelevant to the human world. Hard-schoolers, on the other hand, are convinced that the rational horses do indeed represent an ideal of human behavior, devastating to contemporary humankind. To this argument they invoke Plato, Plutarch, Horace, Temple, and other thinkers Swift is known to have admired. Pedro de Mendez, the virtuous Portuguese sea captain, is shrugged off by the hard school; the soft school, on the other hand, puffs him as Swift's brief but strategically positioned model for human behavior—a role the hard school finds too big for Mendez to play. On the ending, most soft-school critics see Gulliver as ultimately the butt of Swift's satire; hence some soft-schoolers view the entire work as a comedy, affirming the dignity of humanity's middle status and "smiling at the absurdity of the view that can see *only* the Yahoo in man" (Ross, "Final Comedy" 196). For the hard school, however, the impasse described in Gulliver's return home is meant to vex rather than to divert the reader.

In the 1940s and 1950s, the soft school awoke with a vengeance, stimulated partly by pioneering essays on point of view and the satiric persona. The essays of Kathleen Williams are among the clearest representatives of the soft-school position; others include the works listed at the end of this volume by Ross ("Final Comedy"), Tuveson ("Swift"), Monk, Tracy, Kelling, Kallich, Winton, and Ehrenpreis ("Meaning"). Hard-school essays include the pivotal defenses of the Houyhnhnms by Sherburn and Crane ("The Houyhnhnms"), as well as essays by Kelsall, Watkins, Wilson, Rosenheim ("Fifth Voyage"), Suits, Greene ("Education"), Peake ("Coherence"), and others.

Collections of essays on *Gulliver's Travels* are plentiful, but all are decidedly dated (the best of these are Brady; Foster; Tuveson; and the

Norton Critical Edition). Since many teachers will want to include several more recent interpretations, the following is a brief survey of some of the most interesting published after 1965.

The issue of the Yahoos is engaged, on the one hand, by the soft-school suggestion that Christian doctrine renders Swift's Yahoos too extreme to represent humankind (McManmon); on the other, by the hard-school restatement of the "satiric formula" in which the Yahoos do accurately symbolize one side of human nature (Zimansky). Other entries include the (hard) argument against a comforting middle-state view of human nature (Kooroy), both soft- and hard-school etymologies of the Yahoos' tribal name (Zirker, Pyle), and a (mostly hard) analysis of how the theriophilic tradition of preferring animals to human beings contributes to the eternal teasing of book 4 (Gill, "Beast over Man").

On the meaning of the Houyhnhnms, the soft school effectively belittles the horses' economic policies (Wilding, Thorpe, Kelly) (but see Landa's hard-school argument in "The Dismal Science" that the Houyhnhnms' simple agrarian economy rebukes consumer-oriented, luxurious, service-trade-riddled England). They also accuse Gulliver's Houyhnhnm masters of repulsiveness (LaCasce, "Fall"), snobbery (Reichard, "Satiric Snobbery"), snap judgments and superficiality (John H. White), and moral complacency (Thomas), and they compare Gulliver's infatuation with the horses to his delusions about the Struldbruggs (Radner). On the hard-school side, energy goes to identifying presumably unassailable utopias or heroic behavior that resemble Houyhnhnmland, including Horace's Sabine farm (Knowles), the six ideal heroes in book 2, chapter 7 (Kelsall), Temple's *Of Heroic Virtue* (Pierre), the superior Chinese culture (Takase), Plutarch (Halewood), Plato's *Republic* (Reichert). Additional arguments for the horses come from contemporary clichés about the rationality of humanity (Halewood and Levich); from the observation that the Houyhnhnms' sanity is not truly repulsive but merely "insufficiently childish for our tastes" (John Morris); from the understanding that Houyhnhnmland is itself "the thing which is not," expressing not lies but transcendent truths (Philmus, "Swift, Gulliver"). As always, the hard school cautions against weighing trivial faults against the horses, as if they were characters in a psychological novel (Yeomans).

On the role of Pedro de Mendez, the lines have been drawn since Ross, Williams, and other soft-school critics described the kindly captain as "a foil to Gulliver's misanthropy, . . . evidence that Gulliver has gone off the deep end and cannot recover himself from the nightmare view of Yahoo-man" (Ross, "Final Comedy" 193). The insight has been refined a little by Phillipson, who calls Mendez a "halfway house" for Gulliver on his return from confinement to the world outside. The hard-school answer of Conrad Suits has not really been improved upon: "But, what are a few sound apples in a barrelful of rotten ones?" (129).

The soft school has always taken its stand on the misanthropic ending, for the most part, by treating Gulliver as a psychologically whole, novelistic character. They argue that the manifest deterioration of Gulliver's perceptions and morality disqualify his judgments in book 4 (Cook, Reichard, Zimmerman, Sackett, Fitzgerald, Vance, Beauchamp, Otten, Bentman, Fetrow, Trimmer, Pullen). As Steven M. Cohan says, the "power of Gulliver's four imaginary voyages is not that of a satire, but of a fiction" (Cohan 7). On the opposing side, the argument against reading the *Travels* as a novel has never slackened: Gulliver is an instrument of satire, not a psychological character (Smith; Quintana, "Satiric Intent"); he remains plausible, recognizable, only so that the satire may avoid dilution (Greene, "Education"; Moore; Suits).

Some teachers may wish their classes to explore book 4 fully at this level of controversy; others may decide to springboard from a brief treatment of the hard and soft schools to other ways of framing the conflict or of trying to rise beyond it. H. D. Kelling and Steward LaCasce are among those explicitly seeking to resituate the controversy from Clifford's distinctions: the former sees both Houyhnhnms and Yahoos as metaphors, rendering Swift's own opinion of them indeterminable (also Gill, "Man and Yahoo"); the latter casts the main disagreement between criticism based on "philosophic" assumptions concerning the human nature and that based on "theological" assumptions. John Traugott ("Voyage"), Alexander W. Allison, W. B. Carnochan (*Lemuel*), Raymond Bentman, and Peter Steele, among others, urge that any single vision, hard or soft, is too small. Still other analyses, refocusing on the reading experience itself, steered around or through the hard and soft schools' scrimmage line (Dyson; Rawson, "Gentle Reader"; Rudat; Easthope; Nordon; Hassall; Bony). Yet others examined the related issue of indeterminacy of text, interpretation, or both (Philmus, "Swift, Gulliver"; Castle; Holly; Bony; Zimmerman). (For more detail and additional articles, see my *Swift Studies*; also see Stathis; Tobin and Landa.)

Is interpretation of *Gulliver's Travels* a Rorschach test of our students' personal sensitivity to outrage or sense of humor? Perhaps, but it can be far more: a sizing up of methodological assumptions, areas of historical information, knowledge of generic conventions. Teaching through controversy may be a means of approaching those kinds of insights while bringing scholarly and complex contexts to the study of the text of *Gulliver's Travels*.

Using Student Responses
to Teach *Gulliver's Travels*

Frederik N. Smith

We have all felt uncomfortable with several roles we have found ourselves playing at one time or another in the classroom. I refer, for instance, to the guide in the Museum of Literary Classics, shepherding students through this or that salon: "And on your left, *The Rape of the Lock*, and on your right, Swift's masterpiece, *Gulliver's Travels*"; or to the supercritic, the teacher who teaches by telling: "In this passage, Swift is demonstrating his frustration with British politics, which he was much a part of during the reign of Queen Anne. In fact books 1 and 2 may be read as a sort of loose allegory. . . . "

To counter these roles foisted on me, I have, like many other instructors, used a great deal of class discussion, at both the graduate and undergraduate levels; my best classes when I was a student demanded my immediate involvement, and I have tried to re-create this atmosphere in my own classes. But my discussion method was always at odds with the New Critical tweezering my students and I inevitably fell to practicing at some point in every class. My attempts to validate my students' active participation—by encouraging them to respond personally in class and on their papers, by praising responses I found particularly praiseworthy (hoping to establish student models), and by maintaining for myself a relatively low profile—all had to face, finally, the test of a proper reading as demonstrated by the teacher. I exaggerate, of course. But the point I want to make is that in reader-response criticism I have at last found a critical theory that will support the kind of classes I have been teaching all these years. And I have noticed a new liveliness in class discussion. These days I am sure my students sense my conviction when I tell them that discussion is an essential part of the course and that their responses to *Gulliver's Travels* are important to Swift as well as to Smith.

In teaching Swift or any other writer, I have increasingly stressed not the text or the critical interpretation of the text (both static things) so much as the reader's response to the text. "A literary text must therefore be conceived in such a way that it will engage the reader's imagination in the task of working things out for himself," says Wolfgang Iser, "for reading is only a pleasure when it is active and creative" (*Implied Reader* 275). It is easy to substitute "student" for "reader" in this sentence. Employing as a pedagogy the work of Iser, Roman Ingarden, Stanley Fish, Jonathan Culler, and others (conveniently collected by Tompkins and by Suleiman and Crosman), I have found it useful to emphasize in class the sequentiality of texts, the idea of "gaps" or "blanks" left in the text by the author for the reader to fill in, the reader's desire for consistency, and the distinction between a literary "text" (that thing one finds in the library) and a literary "work" (the text plus a reader's reaction to the text). What I have found is that reader-response criticism offers a fresh way to engage students in the process of reading. Such an approach shows them how they themselves help to construct a work; moreover, it deals head-on with that most vexing of student questions: "Why can't I say the book means anything I want it to mean?" One cannot, of course, but why? Because authors intend one meaning and one meaning only? Because you have not yet earned the right to an opinion? Or simply because (as I tell my six-year-old) I say it is impossible? In any case, by asking my students to identify gaps in a text, to describe how they fill in those gaps, and then to point out cues in the text that trigger their responses, I engage them in the text at hand as well as teach them something about the process of reading. No matter how much I encouraged "participation" in my New Critical classroom, the emphasis remained on the text; in my reader-response classroom things are different. The subject matter has shifted from texts alone to texts plus responses to those texts, and I make no secret about our emphasis, even noting on day one that the syllabus, which cites texts only, is misleading.

The teaching of Swift—who encourages yet controls his reader's responses in a masterly way—can in my experience be mightily rejuvenated by the process-oriented model of reading that reader-response criticism has made available. In *A Tale of a Tub* the hiatuses in the text simply draw explicit and humorous attention to the same sorts of readerly concerns that Swift explores far more subtly in *Gulliver's Travels*. With my graduate students, of course, I say exactly this; with my undergraduates I typically allude to Swift's earlier work and jokingly tell them about the paragraphs of asterisks at the peak of the argument. (Analogously, I have had good luck explaining the phenomenology of reading through discussion of the dashes in Emily Dickinson's poetry.)

Even the prefatory documents to *Gulliver's Travels* hint at a text that is not correct or in proper order (see Gulliver's letter) and from which something has been deleted (see Sympson's answer). On the first page (Davis ed.) there is mention of Gulliver's father but none of his mother. Is she dead? Is she unimportant to him? Gulliver makes a voyage or two "into the Levant and some other Parts." What other parts? He marries because he has been "advised to alter my condition." Was this the only reason he married? Then on page 2 we are told: "It would not be proper for some Reasons, to trouble the Reader with the Particulars of our Adventures in those Seas." Why not? What are the reasons? After all, Gulliver in the very next sentence tells us that the crew found itself "in the Latitude of 30 Degrees 2 Minutes South." Of course all travel books are by definition a selection of facts that the traveler considers important or of interest to the reader; Swift, however, has written a book in which supposed facts nearly overwhelm us, although at the same time he has drawn attention to Gulliver's periodic omission of certain things he knows but is choosing not to tell. Swift deliberately makes his reader aware of the process of selection. Gulliver says over and over that he wants to avoid troubling his reader, Swift, on the other hand, wants to trouble his reader from beginning to end. *Gulliver's Travels*, I tell my class, is at least in part a book about the process of reading, and as in any sensitively written literary text, the cues for a correct or incorrect reading are there in the book.

As soon as my students begin to get a feel for Swift's relation with his reader—textual incompleteness employed for ironic purposes—they begin to discover all kinds of examples for themselves. They begin to pay attention to what Gulliver does *not* say: "These false Informations, which I afterwards came to the Knowledge of, by an Accident not proper to mention" (66); "I fell to my Neck in the Hole . . . and coined some Lye not worth remembering, to excuse my self for spoiling my Cloaths" (117); "From this Way of Reasoning the Author drew several moral Applications useful in the Conduct of Life, but needless here to repeat" (137). Why are these things not recorded? How can it be that feet and inches, longitude and latitude and minutes can be deemed important enough to report, but not such matters as these? When Gulliver gives us a do-it-yourselfer's guide to the construction of a miniaturized military field out of sticks and a handkerchief but elects not to reveal the source of false informations, a lie, or useful morals, then we have to wonder about his priorities.

My students notice that Gulliver conceals from the Lilliputians "one private Pocket which escaped the Search" (37) and thus recognize that on his departure the Lilliputian emperor may have reason for a "diligent Search into my Pockets," although there is irony (because Gulliver has not been altogether forthright) in the emperor's appeal to Gulliver's honor not to carry away any of his subjects (78). With a little prodding, students can spot the contradiction in this situation: Gulliver, hiding in the wheat from the approaching Brobdingnagians, thinks (there is an echo of a syllogism here): "For, as human Creatures are observed to be more Savage and cruel in Proportion to their Bulk; what could I expect but to be a Morsel in the Mouth of the first among these enormous Barbarians who should happen to seize me?" (87); on the contrary, the Brobdingnagian recognizes his discomfort and "lifting up the Lappet of his Coat, put me gently into it, and immediately ran along with me to his Master" (88). Swift's reader must make the all-important connection: not all human creatures are as vicious as Europeans!

My students get involved in the text because they sense they can make some contribution to it. More generally, they notice that Gulliver frequently omits any reference to his feelings, that his meticulousness leaves his judgment often unengaged, that his chauvinistic bravado rules out many seemingly demanded acknowledgments that back in England all is not well. They wonder why he fails to point out that the Lilliputian treasurer's wife was too small for him to have intercourse with, and how he can report that in Brobdingnag he was called a "Splacknuck" and not register any shame. They are shocked that he can describe for his Houyhnhnm master the European machinery of war without revealing any distaste whatsoever. By getting my students to pay attention to what is *not* in the text, that is, I can make them conscious of their personal reactions to what *is* there. What they learn, of course, is how to handle Swiftian irony, which works by saying not the opposite of what one means but simply a great deal less. And if they can manage this text, I tell them, then they can manage almost any.

Once the principle is learned, we discuss in class some particular passages of *Gulliver's Travels*, such as that at the end of book 4, chapter 6. The Houyhnhnm master one day flatters Gulliver ("a Compliment which I could not pretend to deserve") by imagining he must be a member of the nobility. Gulliver expresses his "most humble Acknowledgements for the good Opinion he was pleased to conceive of me" but responds that his birth instead "was of the lower Sort" and launches into a long explication of the moral and physical degeneracy of English nobility (256–57).

"Consistency-building," says Iser, "is the indispensable basis for all acts of comprehension. . . . This basic structure is exploited by literary texts in such a way that the reader's imagination can be manipulated and even reoriented" (*Act of Reading* 125). Swift's text here and elsewhere pulls disconcertingly in two directions at once. How is it possible for Gulliver to appreciate his master's compliment and yet hold such disdain for the nobility? The reader struggles to build consistency out of this textual contradiction. Is the inconsistency in Gulliver himself? Are we overhearing a dialogue between persona and author? Or should we simply accept here (without succumbing to the persona game at all) that we are reading a text that is not absolutely synchronized? In class, I welcome attempts to restore a unity at this point, but I stress above all the importance of our reactions; whatever they may be, they become part of Swift's meaning. Indeed, from his or her perspective the reader's response is perhaps the most essential element of the work, for how we deal with its complexity indicates something about how well we might manage similar complexities in or out of texts. If we can remain attentive to how we read *Gulliver's Travels*, we have the possibility of discovering something quite extratextual.

One might ask whether this approach is really so different. Is getting students to hunt for gaps in a text any better than getting them to track down metaphors and symbols? I think so. The difference is between the study of a revered classic that tends to exclude students and the reading of a suddenly accessible text that *requires* the participation of its student-readers. "We actually participate in the text," says Iser, "and this means we are caught up in the very thing we are producing" (*Act of Reading* 127). By emphasizing the reader's responses in the teaching of literature—and Swift's emphasis on the reader makes him especially amenable to this approach—we can restore readers to their rightful role as cocreator with the author. For me as critic, the chief danger is that my criticism will lose touch with my process of reading. For me as teacher, the chief danger is that my teaching will tend to exclude my students' responses. To permit either to happen falsifies the experience of reading; the latter would miss an opportunity for a dynamic class.

One teaching idea. I have recently been experimenting with "reading journals," which require students to record their responses to the assigned texts during the process of reading or immediately thereafter. I am encouraging my students to explore a variety of formats in these journals: double entries, where a fragment of the text is listed on the left side of the page, a response on the right; dialogue entries, where a question is posed about a peculiarly difficult passage, then an answer attempted; or a record of responses of other kinds, such as reactions early, middle, and late in the text, or reactions on first reading, second reading, and so forth. I find that at least students are especially well prepared for class discussions—students seem far more capable of articulating their responses. These journals are also a marvelous storehouse of possible paper topics; one student who had never before read *A Modest Proposal* did a paper on the frustrations a reader feels while moving through the text. But above all, the journal keeping has enabled me to underscore a significant point: meaning in a literary work is the fusion of a text and a response to that text. As I tell my students, their journal entries are an invaluable documentary of their responses, texts themselves, which, studied alongside Swift's text, can get us about as close to his meaning as we are going to get.

Big Men and Little Men, Houyhnhnms and Yahoos: Structural Parallels and Meaning in *Gulliver's Travels*

Peter J. Schakel

Samuel Johnson is said to have dismissed *Gulliver's Travels* with the comment, "When once you have thought of big men and little men, it is very easy to do all the rest" (Boswell 2: 319). Perhaps for a mind like Johnson's, able to compose the speeches delivered the previous day by any member of Parliament on any given topic, it would have been very easy, having thought of big men and little men, to do all the rest. Ordinary mortals, less able to improvise on a given theme, are less quick to downplay Swift's achievement. Perhaps thinking of the big men and little men is, in itself, worthy of admiration. But Johnson's remark leaves unresolved the issue of what "all the rest" includes—parts 1 and 2 only, or 3 and 4 as well? I will suggest here that thinking of the big men and little men may have led Swift to a framework for part 4, or that at any rate reading parts 1 and 2 together provides a model for a reading of part 4. Following that model highlights the greater complexity of part 4 and can be useful in the classroom as providing an entry to the work and initial understanding of its basic structure and themes.

In parts 1 and 2 Gulliver is located physically between the tiny Lilliputians and the giant Brobdingnagians. In Lilliput Gulliver (presumably about six feet tall) finds himself looking at "a human Creature not six Inches high" (Davis ed. 21). In Brobdingnag he is on the other end of the same twelve-to-one ratio: as the farmer brings Gulliver "within three Yards of his Eyes" for a close look, Gulliver dangles "in the Air above sixty Foot from the Ground" (87). The physical proportions make Gulliver a Brobdingnagian to the Lilliputians and a Lilliputian to the Brobdingnagians. Thus he is both Lilliputian and Brobdingnagian, though at the same time he is neither.

The relations suggested by the physical juxtapositions are reinforced by verbal juxtapositions, as part 2 echoes part 1 in idea and expression. For example, in Brobdingnag Gulliver is terrified, when he first sees the giants, because, "as human Creatures are observed to be more Savage and cruel in Proportion to their Bulk; what could I expect but to be a Morsel in the Mouth of the first among these enormous Barbarians who should happen to seize me?" (87). Such an idea comes to his mind, it would seem, because that is exactly what occurred to him in Lilliput—though he forgets that the huge creature there was not savage and cruel:

I took them all in my right Hand, put five of them into my Coat-
pocket; and as to the sixth, I made a Countenance as if I would
eat him alive. The poor Man squalled terribly, and the Colonel
and his Officers were in much Pain, especially when they saw me
take out my Penknife: But I soon put them out of Fear; for,
looking mildly, and immediately cutting the Strings he was
bound with, I set him gently on the Ground, and away he ran. I
treated the rest in the same Manner. (31)

Several other echoes have a similar effect and function:

PART 2	PART 1
I apprehended every Moment that he would dash me against the Ground, as we usually do any little hateful Animal which we have a Mind to destroy. (88)	I confess I was often tempted . . . to seize Forty or Fifty of the first that came in my Reach, and dash them against the Ground. (24)
I had a Table placed upon the same at which her Majesty eat, just at her left Elbow; and a Chair to sit on. (105)	I placed them upon Chairs of State on my Table, just over against me. (64)
The Queen . . . would craunch the Wing of a Lark, Bones and all, between her Teeth, although it were nine Times as large as that of a full-grown Turkey. (106)	I have had a Sirloin so large, that I have been forced to make three Bits of it; but this is rare. My Servants were astonished to see me eat it Bones and all, as in our Country we do the Leg of a Lark. (64)
He was strongly bent to get me a Woman of my own Size, by whom I might propagate the Breed: But I think I should rather have died than undergone the Disgrace of leaving a Posterity to be kept in Cages like tame Canary Birds. (139)	I took with me six Cows and two Bulls alive, with as many Yews and Rams, intending to carry them into my own Country, and propagate the Breed. . . . I would gladly have taken a Dozen of the Natives; but this was a thing the Emperor would by no Means permit. (78)

The Lilliputians and Brobdingnagians resemble human beings in
physical appearance (size apart) and in personal and social characteristics, so that Gulliver inevitably falls between them. The relation
between each species and Gulliver (or humankind) is essentially
straightforward and unambiguous: The Lilliputians appear to be
attractive and likable but in reality are aggressive and nasty; the
reader readily recognizes their flaws, their resemblances to humans,
and the unfavorable ethical model they present. The Brobdingnagians
are fearsome in appearance, but the king, at least (unlike the greedy
and insensitive farmer who first owns Gulliver and the spiteful and

envious dwarf), presents a favorable ethical model for those who will make an effort to attain it.

Thus Gulliver finds himself in a situation that challenges his identity and values. He is forced by his situation to ask the eternal questions, "Who am I?" and "What am I doing here?" Is he a Lilliputian—physically dainty and beautiful but a tiny, insignificant speck, petty, vicious, and full of pride, as he appears in Brobdingnag? Is he a Brobdingnagian—physically unattractive but greathearted, magnanimous, and gracious, as he appears in Lilliput? His plea that he is neither Lilliputian nor Brobdingnagian but human, though true, is little comfort, for as such he is afflicted with few of the best and most of the worst traits of both.

LILLIPUTIANS	◄— GULLIVER —►	BROBDINGNAGIANS
yes	physically similar?	yes
as himself—no	morally, socially,	in actions—no
as humanity—yes	politically similar?	in capability—yes

Swift's placement of Gulliver—and humankind—physically and morally between the Lilliputians and the Brobdingnagians is not an abstract exercise in definitions. That placement creates enormous tensions that pull desperately at Gulliver—and readers of *Gulliver*—from various sides. They do not pull Gulliver apart, but only because their implications have not yet sunk in far enough—as they will after a later journey, recounted in part 4, presents him with an even greater dilemma.

Such physical and moral tensions are not evident in part 3, however—which may explain to a considerable extent why that part (written after part 4) is usually considered less interesting than the others. There is a pause in the emotional buildup, which gives a temporary relief before the final heightening of tension and perhaps helps intensify it when it comes. Gulliver is never physically in danger in Laputa, Balnibarbi, Luggnagg, or Glubbdubdrib, as he is in both Lilliput and Brobdingnag, so the reader is less emotionally involved with him. He is mainly an onlooker: the satire is directed rarely at him (except in the Struldbrugg episode) but more often at the foolishness of others all about him. In particular, he feels no tension regarding his identity; throughout, he seems to know who he is and seems indeed to be more self-possessed and sane than most of the people he encounters. As a result, the satire, trenchant and continuingly applicable though it is, to the twentieth century as well as the eighteenth, has less appeal and makes less impact than that of the other three parts.

Part 4 follows the same structure as parts 1 and 2 but compresses it into a single book and splits it up into a more complex configuration. Gulliver touches the Houyhnhnms on the one side and the Yahoos on the other, yet is not quite in touch with either; but in this part, the emphasis shifts from the external to the internal, from appearance and behavior to essential being. Gulliver finds himself between the Houyhnhnms and Yahoos, not because of physical appearance (though that creates part of the tension he experiences) but because that which makes him human is divided between the two species: he connects with the Yahoos in physical-emotional nature, while he connects with the Houyhnhnms in rational-moral nature.

YAHOOS	←—— GULLIVER ——→	HOUYHNHNMS
yes	physically-emotionally similar?	no
no	rationally-morally similar?	in actions—no in capability—yes

He is both Yahoo and Houyhnhnm, yet is neither. He is trapped in the same tension as in books 1 and 2, and so, with him, is the rest of humankind.
- Although Gulliver is preoccupied with his physical resemblance to the Yahoos—"I exactly resembled [the Yahoos] in my Head, Hands and Face" (235); "it was plain I must be a perfect *Yahoo*" (237); "I could no longer deny, that I was a real *Yahoo*, in every Limb and Feature, since the Females had a natural Propensity to me as one of their own Species" (267)—that is less important to the Houyhnhnms than the difference indicated by evidences of reason in him. More important than either, however, are similarities in temperament and behavior between his race and the Yahoos. Gulliver's Houyhnhnm master mentions on page 260 that "he found as near a Resemblance in the Disposition" of Yahoo and human minds, and on page 262 he notes "what Parity there was in our Natures." That is, in addition to the accidental physical similarities, humans resemble Yahoos in emotional attitudes, a much more significant dimension.

In chapters 4–6 Swift forces the reader to look at the misuse of emotions, and the effects of such abuses, in European society. Gulliver's account is exaggerated, of course, but that does not negate the charges. There is truth behind what he says about the effects of greed, desire for power, ambition, and lust, and in those traits human beings resemble the Yahoos. As chapter 7 shows the Yahoos fighting over shiny pebbles, squabbling over food they don't need, getting drunk on the juice of a root, it becomes a mirror providing humankind a reflection of itself. Human beings are Yahoos whenever they fail to use reason to rise above such behavior. Significantly, they even fall below Yahoo status when they misuse reason: "He [Gulliver's Houyhnhnm master] looked upon us as a Sort of Animals to whose Share, by what Accident he could not conjecture, some small Pittance of *Reason* had fallen, whereof we made no other Use than by its Assistance to aggravate our *natural* Corruptions, and to acquire new ones which Nature had not given us" (259); "I expected every Moment, that my Master would accuse the *Yahoos* of those unnatural Appetites in both Sexes, so common among us. But Nature it seems hath not been so expert a Schoolmistress; and these politer Pleasures are entirely the Productions of Art and Reason, on our Side of the Globe" (264).

Contrariwise, Gulliver is not like the Houyhnhnms physically: they are horses. Swift turned the logic-book definition of "man" as *animal rationale* and of "horse" as *animal irrationale* upside down and made the horses reasonable creatures (Crane, "Houyhnhnms" 245–50). Their reason, unlike human reason, is not mingled, obscured, or discolored by passion and interest, so it "strikes you with immediate Conviction" (267). Just as Gulliver falls short of the apparently perfect moral attitudes of the Brobdingnagian king, so he falls short of the wholly rational nature of the Houyhnhnms.

But, as Gulliver resembles the king in his capacity for morality, so human beings are like Houyhnhnms in that they have and are capable of using reason. Swift makes that point, seriously or not, in an often-quoted letter to Pope, 29 September 1725: "I have got Materials Towards a Treatis [the *Travels*] proving the falsity of that Definition *animal rationale*; and to show it should be only *rationis capax*" (*Correspondence* 3: 103). Gulliver's Houyhnhnm master, using words that resemble that letter, was "more astonished at my Capacity for Speech and Reason, than at the Figure of my Body" (237)—of course that is the whole point. The Houyhnhnms and humans are reasoning creatures, and humans often pride themselves on their reasonableness ("You're being unreasonable, though I'm being perfectly reasonable myself"). Part 4 shows, in reply to such pride, how far short human beings fall of using reason as they could. Chapters 8–9 describe Houyhnhnm society and provide a "perfectly reasonable" standard by which Europeans can evaluate their own use of reason. The Houyhnhnms' "grand Maxim is, to cultivate *Reason*, and to be wholly governed by it" (267); likewise, humans have at least "some small Pittance of *Reason*" to cultivate (259), and to a considerable extent reason is indeed "sufficient to govern [direct, guide, regulate the conduct or actions of] a *Rational* Creature" (259). Gulliver, however, finds that he "must freely confess, that the many Virtues of those excellent *Quadrupeds* placed in opposite View to human Corruptions, had so far opened mine Eyes, and enlarged my Understanding, that I began to view the Actions and Passions of Man in a very different Light" (258). So too readers are to view their actions and attitudes more clearly and honestly, by comparing them to Houyhnhnm life, but the comparisons here are not so easy and obvious as they were in parts 1 and 2.

They are more difficult because the Houyhnhnms are to some extent to be emulated, to some extent not, and the line dividing the positive and negative is not obvious or fixed. Clearly, neither ungoverned passions nor passionless reason is something for which human beings should strive: Gulliver's identification of the human shape with reasonlessness and equine shape with pure reason reduces each extreme to a caricature and thus invalidates each as a possible ideal. But the lines separating the untenable extremes from the middle area where reason is energized by, and governs, emotion are not defined or definable. It is also clear that one extreme is less untenable than the other: pure reason comes across as less dangerous than pure passion. Though Houyhnhnm life in toto is not an ideal for humans, within their lives and society are qualities and attitudes desirable for human life and society. Humans could learn from the Houyhnhnms, for example, to be moderate and composed and to order family and community life in a more simple and sensible way than it is now ordered. Part 4 thrusts upon readers of Swift's day and ours the most wrenching perplexities that confront them, morally, socially, personally: of human cruelty and violence perpetrated on others, of greed and waste, of depravity and perversion; it sets out qualities of temperateness, benevolence, and reasonableness, as exhibited by the Houyhnhnms generally, to provide guidelines for acceptable human behavior; but it leaves readers to work out the proper mix of emotion with reason and application of the guidelines to specific situations. Humankind, thus, is caught in an unresolved tension, being partially Yahoo and partially Houyhnhnm, facing the necessity and danger of the physical and emotional on the one hand and of the ethereal and rational on the other. Thus Gulliver in part 4, drawn toward both the Yahoos and the Houyhnhnms, is living out a dramatized definition of the human condition.

For Gulliver, however, the tension he experiences is unbearable, and he attempts to resolve it by reducing the situation to abstractions. He is pushed by physical resemblance toward identifying with the Yahoos but resists that pressure because he finds the creatures repellent in behavior. He tries to identify with the Houyhnhnms because their use of reason appeals to him but is held back by his physical dissimilarity and his feelings of inferiority. As in parts 1 and 2, where Gulliver misses the point of the nastiness and viciousness evident in the Lilliputians and the generosity, magnanimity, and reasonableness of the Brobdingnagian king, so he misses the point in part 4 and isolates the physical aspects of both Houyhnhnms and Yahoos as his sole concern. Instead of seeing and emulating those things in the Houyhnhnms that he could learn and improve from, Gulliver tries to become a horse (279) and back in England buys two horses and spends four hours a day talking to them. And because of his revulsion from the Yahoos, he ends up hating his own species on account of its physical similarity to Yahoos (not the emotional-behavioral similarity, which should cause him to be revolted). Thus he is utterly unable to distinguish between savages (in chapter 11), who attempt to kill him, and the magnanimous Portuguese captain Don Pedro de Mendez, who treats him so well. He cannot stand the touch of his wife and finds the sight and smell of his children revolting. And he hates himself because of his physical nature, as is evident in his determination "to behold my Figure often in a Glass, and thus if possible habituate my self by Time to tolerate the Sight of a human Creature" (295). A mirror ought to give one a clear look at, or understanding of, oneself; Gulliver looks in a mirror, however, not to see who he is, not to understand himself or his race fully, but to accustom himself to Yahoos (that is, to accustom himself to the sight, the physical appearance, of a human creature). Having isolated the physical elements of the Yahoos and Houyhnhnms and fixed his attention on them, he is unable to grasp either species, or humankind, or himself, as total beings. The tension he felt in parts 1 and 2 has greatly intensified and become destructive.

The tension has intensified for the reader as well. In parts 1 and 2 the structure led readers to identify with Gulliver's perspective: since he was the only human available, a sensible, decent one, that was inevitable. In part 4 that structure is complicated as readers initially continue to identify with him, begin to feel comfortable with his abstractions of Yahoo and Houyhnhnm qualities, then gradually discover that his way of escaping the human dilemma is unacceptable. A new tension is created as readers are forced to disassociate themselves from Gulliver and thus are thrust back into the dilemma he was endeavoring to escape. The *Travels* shows, in the end, that the tensions described in parts 1, 2, and 4 are inescapable; they are part of what it is to be human. Nothing in Gulliver's journeys—not Gulliver himself, not the Brobdingnagians (for though the king is admirable, few ordinary citizens are shown to be so), not the Houyhnhnms— provides a single, simple model for avoiding such tensions. Through its structural patterns, *Gulliver's Travels* does, however, offer guidelines by which individuals, torn as they are between big men and little men, Yahoos and Houyhnhnms, can mold behavior and ideals acceptable to themselves and for society as a whole.

The Multiple Identities of Gulliver's "Reader"

Janet E. Aikins

Each time I teach *Gulliver's Travels*, I am surprised at the intensity of student response to the narrator of the fourth voyage. No matter what scholarly explanations I provide (Carnochan, "Complexity"; Crane, "Houyhnhnms"; Stone; Suits), I never entirely calm the outrage at the Gulliver who abhors the stench of his own family:

> By the end of the fourth section, I had really lost quite a bit of respect for Gulliver. . . . I think [he] was wrong to totally condemn his own race. . . .

> I felt [it] was not a way in which he ought to talk of his own country. . . . In part 4, Gulliver even rejected his own flesh and blood. He became cold and unaffectionate like the "horses."

> It is with the Houyhnhnms and Yahoos that Gulliver . . . takes the dive into despicability. It is also the section that is most confusing; it's not really enjoyable reading . . . , perhaps because it hits too close to home. . . . [If] we, like Gulliver, identify too closely with [the Yahoos] we have to believe that we are despicable too.

> The character [of Gulliver], once amusing, is now disturbing. He became bitter and he dwelt on the negative aspects of society. . . . I grant that he did make valid points but it is uncomfortable to be constantly reminded of them.

Whatever coherence they may see in part 4, students persist in feeling "depressed," "confused," "uncomfortable," and "disturbed" after reading it.

Such responses have led me to examine a feature of Swift's text that is crucial to its power as satire—namely, the multiple identity of its "implied Readers." Critics have paid increasing attention to the reading experience in the *Travels* (Bony; Brady, "Vexations"; Kinsley; Oakleaf; Probyn, *Art*; Uphaus), but they have overlooked this odd phenomenon. In the classroom it is helpful to show that Swift posits not one but at least three kinds of "readers" within the narrative, all different in their implied responses to Gulliver, for much of our "confusion" in part 4 results from this peculiarity. I therefore ask my undergraduates to perform two tasks. First, they must write a brief but honest description of their personal feelings about the Gulliver of the fourth volume. Second, each person must list a variety of instances in which Gulliver talks to the reader, describes him or her, or makes implied assumptions about the reader's attitudes or identity. By comparing lists, the class uncovers a startling range of inconsistency in the assumed character of the "Reader" throughout the text. The point is to suggest various hypotheses about the audience Swift may have imagined he was addressing as he composed the four voyages.

Obviously every author contemplates a potential reader, and Swift was no exception. In the 1762 collection of his works, the editor recorded an anecdote about his approach to writing. Swift allegedly insisted:

> That the Editor should attend him early every Morning, or when most convenient, to read to him, that the Sounds might strike the Ear, as well as the Sense the Understanding, and had always two Men Servants present for this Purpose; and when he had any Doubt, he would ask them the Meaning of what they heard? Which, if they did not comprehend, he would alter and amend, until they understood it perfectly well, and then would say, *This will do*; *for, I write to the Vulgar, more than to the Learned.*
> (*Works*, Faulkner ed. 1: vii)

This anecdote hints that Swift thought deeply about his readers and valued their responses, however simple and immediate those responses might be.

In many of his letters, Swift appears aware of the imagined recipient as a vital presence (*Correspondence* 2: 36, 464; Ehrenpreis, "Swift's Letters"). When he published Sir William Temple's correspondence, he praised it on the grounds that we gain a rich knowledge of the people to whom Temple wrote merely by observing his style of addressing them. The importance of a "felt" sense of audience is also implied in one of Swift's most celebrated remarks about the *Travels*: "I tell you after all that I do not hate Mankind, it is vous autres who hate them because you would have them reasonable Animals, and are Angry for being disappointed. I have always rejected that Definition and made another of my own" (*Correspondence* 3: 118). These words are often quoted as evidence either for or against the supposed misanthropy of Swift's satires, yet they also suggest an important aesthetic principle: according to the need of the moment, writers should freely attribute whatever traits they wish to potential readers, whether fairly or not. Swift articulated a related idea in a letter of advice to a friend: "expect no more from Man than such an Animal is capable of, and you will every day find my Description of Yahoos more resembling. You should think and deal with every Man as a Villain, without calling him so, or flying from him, or vaulting him less"

(*Correspondence* 3: 94). As we shall see, Gulliver often applies this approach to the readers of his narrative; he mentally exaggerates the attributes he assumes we possess and treats us accordingly, knowing all the while that his assumptions are often untenable. If we can understand the confusion of a man who is treated "as a villain" without being called so, we can begin to explain our perplexed response to Swift's text.

At the start of the *Travels*, the "Publisher" is the first to practice this ploy. In the address "to the Reader" he explains that in his abridgment of the nautical passages, "I was resolved to fit the Work as much as possible to the general Capacity of Readers," as if he were certain what such capacities might be. However, in the next sentence he withdraws his assurance: "if my own Ignorance in Sea-Affairs shall have led me to commit some Mistakes, I alone am answerable for them: And if any Traveller hath a Curiosity to see the whole Work at large, as it came from the Hand of the Author, I will be ready to gratify him" (Davis ed. xxxviii). The first sentence assumes that the "general Capacity" of readers is clearly identifiable, while the second modestly acknowledges such assumptions to be mere hypotheses. The letter to Cousin Sympson multiplies the complication. Within it, Gulliver says that he has sent his cousin certain corrections to be inserted "if ever there should be a second Edition," and he adds a peculiar qualification: "I cannot stand to them, but shall leave that Matter to my judicious and candid Readers, to adjust it as they please" (xxxv). We realize that Swift is being facetious; nevertheless, by speaking these words, Gulliver creates a hypothetical "judicious and candid Reader" whose presence all actual readers must confront, just as they must deal with the various voices of Gulliver himself. We are forced to consider what it would indeed mean to "adjust" *Gulliver's Travels* "as [we] please." Obviously there is no answer to the question, but it is most useful for students to ponder since Swift so eagerly invites our perplexity.

Because *Gulliver's Travels* urges at least three distinct modes of reader response, it is fundamentally unlike many other books. Typically, when we read, we assume that the narrator addresses the reader as a consistent entity. The very concept of "narration" assumes that variations in the tale will arise from shifts in the point of view of the speaker, not from changes in the listener. *Gulliver's Travels* oddly reverses this assumption.

We practice the first mode of "listening" when we employ Edward Rosenheim's definition of satire as "*an attack by means of a manifest fiction upon discernible historic particulars*" (Rosenheim, *Swift* 31). That is, Swift implies connections between events described within the *Travels* and recognizable events in the real world; we identify

Flimnap as a satiric portrait of Walpole, and we notice that the conflict between Lilliput and Blefuscu alludes to the historic disputes between England and France. By exploring such relations, critics have effectively although not exhaustively accounted for part 1 as a political allegory (Harth, "Problem" 545; Lock). Spotting the historical parallels involves our evaluating the actual world. When we respond in this way, we tacitly assume that Gulliver does not really exist but that he is a persona or tool of the satire. We laugh at Swift's blatant artifice when Gulliver pretends to talk to us directly, inserting such unnecessary prompts as "The Reader may remember . . ." (39).

Swift's method is treacherous, however, for at other points the same sort of phrase demands a second, radically different mode of response. For example, after describing his capture by the Lilliputians, his arms, legs, and hair fastened to the ground and small human creatures running up and down his body, Gulliver says, "I lay all this while, as the Reader may believe, in great Uneasiness" (6). The phrase "as the Reader may believe" is as artificial as "The Reader may remember," yet precisely because we can "believe" or relate to Gulliver's uncomfortable situation, our response is of a radically different order. Here we feel in league with the speaker. The visual image of having one's hair and limbs tied down and small creatures crawling over one's flesh creates an undeniable uneasiness in all of us. This is the Gulliver of the "cartoon version" that our students all remember.

In such instances, we are willing to be included in a collective "we." The phenomenon occurs repeatedly throughout the *Travels*, sometimes with a distinct oddity in the allegiance that Gulliver creates. For example, we find ourselves accepting a designation as Englishmen when he expresses indignation at the king of Brobdingnag's contempt for human grandeur: "my Colour came and went several Times, with Indignation to hear our noble Country, the Mistress of Arts and Arms, the Scourge of *France*, the Arbitress of *Europe*, the Seat of Virtue, Piety, Honour and Truth, the Pride and Envy of the World, so contemptuously treated" (91). Whether or not we are English, we tacitly assent to a shared perspective with Gulliver, while at the same time strongly disagreeing with his blind admiration for "our" country. With a similar eagerness to overlook a few facts, we chuckle in assent when Gulliver says that the Lilliputians write "aslant from one Corner of the Paper to the other, like Ladies in *England*" (41), as if we had personally shared Gulliver's observation of an affected style of writing among English women. Even if we cannot sympathize with his male attack on female affectation, we at least acknowledge that a certain type of man will indeed hold a disparaging opinion of women's writing and will make fun of it. Clearly, these reactions are not consciously developed views that we hold with any seriousness, for the illusion is dispelled the moment we contemplate it. Nevertheless, the pressure of Gulliver's words quietly elicits responses like the ones that I have sketched. Students themselves will supply abundant examples.

Our willing inclusion in Gulliver's "us" involves extreme feelings, however momentary, of either sympathy with Gulliver or alienation from him. We are thereby drawn into the fiction, for if we react at all to Gulliver's portrayal of "our" world, as he calls it, we have tacitly assented to the "truth" of the *Travels* and to the existence of Gulliver, fictional though we know him to be. Thus, a vital difference between the first and second "implied reader response" is that while the first assumes that Gulliver is a fictional character, a tool of the satire, the second is tantamount to accepting Gulliver as an actual person (Sacks 32).

The third mode of implied response differs in still another way, for it is prompted by the "Reader" whom Gulliver addresses directly in the text. This figure is a kind of phantom who never speaks and whose identity changes radically from moment to moment, depending on the descriptive adjectives that Gulliver employs. For example, the "Reader" is at various points "candid," "indulgent," "gentle," "judicious," good at understanding the ideas of the Lilliputians even when Gulliver cannot, possessed with a capable imagination, likely to be "diverted" by details of domestic life, someone who does not always wish to be "troubled," and so forth. When all the adjectives are considered together, a complete or coherent description of the "Reader's character" does not emerge, yet because of their specificity we cannot simply dismiss them as jokes on the artifice of the text.

Each of these miniatures demands a local response from actual readers, and every member of the class will have an opinion. For example, when Gulliver assumes that the reader will be "curious" about the exact size, shape, and look of the nursing mother's breast in Brobdingnag, we are forced to consider whether or not he is right about us. He says, "I must confess no Object ever disgusted me so much as the Sight of her monstrous Breast, which I cannot tell what to compare with, so as to give the curious Reader an Idea of its Bulk, Shape and Colour" (75). By the delayed placement of the term "curious Reader" within the sentence, Gulliver gives us sufficient time to become curious about the details of the breast, so that we are then embarrassed when he unexpectedly attributes a curiosity to us rather than to himself. He does not call us prurient; instead, he simply assumes that we are and behaves accordingly, causing us literally to blush. At each of our encounters with the "Reader" a dual process occurs. We partially own up to Gulliver's accuracy in guessing our thoughts, and we simultaneously disown at least a portion of the attributed traits. In this instance, for example, we may be curious not about the breast but rather about Gulliver's obvious fear of it as an exaggerated emblem of female sexuality. As we move through the text, the "Reader" gradually becomes an object of our derision or disdain, for we are strongly inclined to distinguish ourselves from this phantom whom Gulliver claims to know so well.

Every actual reader of Swift's text practices all three of the listening modes that I have described, and the differences among them appear most clearly if we think of them as three sorts of "implied readers" that the text forces us to become. The first is a bodiless figure whose one identifiable trait is the capacity to recognize allusions and parallels between the lands Gulliver explores and the actual world. The second is a slightly less shadowy figure whose existence is implied by Gulliver's use of the pronoun *us* and who thereby appears to share the narrator's cultural and national heritage. Unlike either of these two, the third implied reader defines himself or herself in relation to the "Reader," who possesses a series of ever-changing but highly specific traits.

In addition to the three modes of response, there is yet another reason for student confusion in part 4: in the final volume Gulliver is an alien in disguise, rather like a Houyhnhnm who seems to be only a horse. Even the most alert reader is unlikely to notice until well into part 4 that the narrator's voice has become a new and unpleasant one. We feel glimmerings of the realization as we hear Gulliver describe humankind with less and less sympathy, but we are aghast when we see Gulliver's final treatment of the kind Don Pedro and of his own family. Our progression through the first three volumes has lulled us into complacency, so the disorientation we experience at the eventual discovery of Gulliver's bitterness is like his own "Horror and Astonishment" at discovering a "perfect human Figure" in the features of a Yahoo (213-214). This sly stroke is Swift's ultimate statement about "unwary Readers."

To see why, it is useful to examine the letter to Cousin Sympson, which explicitly attacks readers who have failed to correct the world's ills in response to the lessons of *Gulliver's Travels*. Gulliver complains that the "Reformations" that were "plainly deducible from the Precepts delivered in my Book" have not been put into practice (xxxv). He uses this letter not only to attack the ineffectual reader but to comment on the veracity of his tale and to insist that "the Truth immediately strikes ever Reader with Conviction" (xxxvi). Oddly enough, this same embittered Gulliver complains later on that travel narratives easily abuse the "Credulity" of the "unwary Reader" and expresses his "great Disgust against this Part of Reading" (275), as if the truth did *not* possess the power to "strike" us with conviction as he first declared. What then does it mean to be Captain Gulliver's "Reader with Conviction"? Is this a good or a bad trait? And why does Swift introduce a doubt about Gulliver's integrity in close juxtaposition with his complaint that readers failed to respond to his book as a truthful and explicit directive to change the world? I would suggest that Swift's purpose is to make us not merely active readers, as Uphaus argues, but vigilant ones—unlike the unfortunate "Maid of Honour" who fell asleep while reading a romance (39). He seeks to startle, to "strike" us out of our daze, like a Flapper in Laputa.

The difficulty of deciding the "Truth . . . with conviction" arises often in the *Travels* (33, 51, 55, 63, 70-71, 80, 130, 170, 220, 251) and culminates in an amusing allegorical joke in part 4. The presence of Robert Purefoy ("pure faith") in Gulliver's last doomed vessel is Swift's gentle signal to the "unwary Reader" to pay attention. Purefoy is a young physician whom Gulliver enlists to replace himself on his final voyage, since he has "grown weary of a Surgeon's Employment at Sea" (205). Swift implies that "pure faith" or strength of conviction is dangerous, for we next hear the story of the tragic drowning of Captain Pocock. We are told that although he was "an honest Man, and a good Sailor" he was "a little too positive in his own Opinions, which was the Cause of his Destruction" (205). Here Swift hints that although we have become experienced readers of *Gulliver's Travels* by the time we reach part 4, we would do well to question our own "conviction" or positive opinions about this narrative. Physician Purefoy urges the moral healing of the reader. His name ironically signals that we are about to be drowned by being "a little too positive in our own opinions," for at the very moment when we feel we know Gulliver best, we fail to hear the new, bitter tone in his voice.

The multiple identities of the "implied Reader" thus make *Gulliver's Travels* an especially effective vehicle for heightening student sensitivity to the importance of reader reaction. Too often, undergraduates want to be told the "true meaning" of a particular literary work, a tendency all too strong in the highly referential world of satire. *Gulliver's Travels* is a book about which there is, in this special sense, no truth to be told. Rather, it demands that its readers, whether new or experienced, "Vulgar" or "Learned," take their own responses seriously and examine them as a contributing part of the text.

Teaching *Gulliver's Travels*

John F. Sena

It is universally acknowledged that *Gulliver's Travels* is a literary masterpiece. What might not be as readily acknowledged is that *Gulliver's Travels* is also a pedagogical masterpiece. For students, it is a joy to read. The narrative is lively and exciting, the prose is accessible, and the issues raised are often ones they care about. One does not have to persuade students to read the book; they have generally heard so much about the *Travels* that they want to experience it for themselves. The *Travels* also encourages instructors to be imaginative and creative in their teaching. Its variety and complexity invite us to pursue various pedagogical techniques and multiple critical approaches. I wish to emphasize this latter point. I have found employing diverse approaches—generic, historical, psychological, biographical, New Critical, and interdisciplinary—to be an effective means of explicating the *Travels*, while providing the additional advantage of permitting students to observe, experience, and test the strengths and limitations of various critical biases.

To establish a generic context for reading *Gulliver's Travels*, I generally spend two or three class periods discussing the nature and dynamics of satire. In our discussion, we spend time exploring the aggressiveness of laughter. I have them read Henri Bergson's "Laughter: An Essay on the Meaning of the Comic" in its entirety and excerpts on laughter from Hobbes's *Leviathan* and Freud's *Wit and Its Relation to the Unconscious*. We explore these theories in cinematic and television satires (e.g., Chaplin's *The Tramp* and *Modern Times, All in the Family*), contemporary jokes, and myriads of much better examples supplied by the students. Discussing the nature and effects of laughter and of the literary techniques that elicit laughter provides a useful context for reading *Gulliver's Travels* as well as other eighteenth-century satires. Students have little difficulty, for instance, in seeing the theories of Bergson, Hobbes, and Freud embodied in the laughter that Gulliver constantly provokes from the Brobdingnagians. Bergson's remark that laughter often involves "[s]omething mechanical encrusted on the living . . . " (84), applied to the intellectual rigidity of Gulliver, makes them more aware of the extent to which he is being satirized by Swift. Our theoretical discussion on laughter also allows them to grasp some of the cruxes of the *Travels*. Bergson's belief that laughter necessitates a "momentary anaesthesia of the heart" (64), for example, provides them with a basis for understanding their responses to the concluding chapters of book 4. If students feel sympathy for

Gulliver, they may respond to his forced return in somber, even tragic terms. If they believe that Swift has deliberately used various strategies to separate us from Gulliver, they tend to conclude that the author wishes us to laugh at his protagonist. By understanding the psychological basis of laughter and the conditions that must be present to evoke laughter, students can better formulate a "reading" of this episode—and numerous others—and articulate the bases of their judgments without resorting to vague, impressionistic "feelings."

From an analysis of the elements and dynamics of satire and laughter, I generally proceed to a discussion of generic issues. To what genre does *Gulliver's Travels* belong? Do we define genre in terms of the objective, the techniques, or the structure of a work? When we say that the *Travels* is a satire, is that a generic description? Is *Gulliver's Travels* in the generic tradition of travel literature? In general, students are unfamiliar with the style and conventions of seventeenth- and eighteenth-century travel works, so I approach this question by having them describe the prose style of book 1. The sentences, they observe, often follow a subject-verb-object sequence and lack modulation in tone; nouns are generally concrete, while precise distances and physical measurements abound. These observations, as well as Gulliver's comments on travel writers, help them begin to understand the conventions of travel works that Swift is both adopting and satirizing.

The generic question that raises the most heated debate by far is whether *Gulliver's Travels* is a novel. Is there in the *Travels*, for instance, the sense of the causality, of one event's leading logically to the next, that we usually associate with the novel? Does Lemuel Gulliver share the complexity and consistency that characterizes the protagonist of a novel? Are the kinds of subplots or analogous actions that one finds in, say, a Dickens novel present in *Gulliver's Travels*? Are, indeed, causality, complexity and consistency of character, and subplots essential to the novel? While this discussion provokes disagreement, it forces students to examine their critical assumptions and expectations about genre. Most students, by the way, conclude that whatever they should call *Gulliver's Travels*, they should not call it a novel.

While we are discussing satire and the novel, I have my students write a two-page "position paper" on the *Travels*. This assignment is totally open-ended: I ask them to write about anything—from a paragraph to an entire book, from a minor character to a major theme—that strikes them as significant. When they submit those papers to me, we spend one class session engaged in "show and tell." I randomly call on individuals to give the class a two- or three-minute précis of their papers. After doing this for years, I am still amazed at the variety of their observations. Often these are influenced by events occurring outside of the classroom: the Watergate scandal prompted discussion of how absolute power corrupts absolutely, or how politicians corrupt language in book 1; our involvement in El Salvador prompted expositions on the abuses of governmental power; *Planet of the Apes* movies inspired heartfelt responses on value systems and prejudices appearing in book 4.

After this introductory class on the *Travels*, we undertake each book in turn. I approach book 1 historically: I provide the class with a brief description of the eighteenth-century events and personalities reflected in that book. My greatest problem is determining how much history is enough. At what point have we made literature a function of time? While I want to provide students with a historical context for reading book 1, I have found that most undergraduates have only a passing interest in the War of the Spanish Succession, the Harley ministry, and the alleged treason of Bolingbroke. As a partial solution to this problem, I have devised a two-page handout that lists on the left-hand side an event from book 1 and opposite it a brief historical analogue to that event. This, combined with the notes in Louis Landa's edition of the *Travels*—notes that I consider informative and balanced—provides undergraduates with a fairly comprehensive commentary on the events of book 1. It also allows me to spend more time deriving principles of political conduct from the book and having students interpolate events from book 1 in their own terms.

I begin book 2 by requiring a brief New Critical explication of that book based on tracing words for physical distress, such as *hurt*, *pain*, and *injury*. This leads us to a discussion of the concept of the body in book 2, and that becomes the organizing principle for our approach. We talk about the vulnerability and weakness of Gulliver's body as emblematic of the vulnerability and weakness of human nature (Fussell 127-135). Students often remark on Gulliver's imprisonment in the box used for carrying him as a metaphor for the limitations imposed by humankind's physical nature, while some will see an existential dimension to Gulliver's uncertain existence in Brobdingnag.

We also discuss the antiromantic view of the body expressed in the maids-of-honor episode. At this point I have them read several of Swift's scatological poems—"A Beautiful Young Nymph Going to Bed," "The Progress of Beauty," "The Lady's Dressing Room"—on a similar theme. Swift's use of scatology now surfaces and becomes our focus for at least one period, frequently more. While students generally applaud his efforts to convince his readers of the impermanence of the body and of a love based on it, there always remains a hard core in every class who will, while approving of his objectives, argue that the intensity and amount of his scatology are gratuitous, that attributing them to his effort to shock his readers is too simple and facile. Despite my attempts to point out the need to place Swift's scatology in a historical context, or the danger of reading his satire with contemporary sensibilities, or that Swift is trying to demonstrate that beauty is not even skin deep, I generally fail to change anyone's mind.

Our discussion of scatology leads us, in turn, to reflect on Swift and parts of book 2 in psychological terms. Invariably a student will ask what Swift meant when, at the end of Gulliver's visit to the dressing room of the maids of honor, he has Gulliver declare: "The handsomest among these maids of honour, a pleasant frolicsome girl of sixteen, would sometimes set me astride upon one of her nipples, with many other tricks, wherein the reader will excuse me for not being over particular." This passage—along with the description several paragraphs later of Gulliver in a boat (a little man in a boat), Gulliver's rocking back and forth in his boat with the frog, and Gulliver's dousing with slime—generally stimulates students to talk about these events in terms of suppressed libidos, wish fulfillment, and masturbation fantasies. Most students are psychologically sophisticated enough to see both a basis for speculation and the foolishness of trying to make conclusive judgments about Swift's sexuality from the evidence available.

This discussion leads us to attempt a biographical approach to the significance of the body in book 2. We talk briefly about Swift's illnesses—Ménière's syndrome, orbital cellulitis, cerebral arteriosclerosis. They can see a relation between a man whose body was the source of exquisite pain and a character in a fictional work whose body is constantly causing him distress and agony.

Book 3 presents several pedagogical problems for me because of its structural and thematic looseness. Students tend to find it disunified and fragmented, occasionally theorizing that Swift had simply sundry observations he wanted to make and issues he wanted to raise that would not fit into the other books. While I am not convinced that this view is totally erroneous, I try to provide a conceptual unity to the book by discussing it in terms of *la puta* ("the whore"). We talk about the various ways people prostitute their talents: politicians who do not provide for the needs of their people, professors who employ mechanical contraptions rather than intelligence to write books, scholars who are not interested in enlightening, and, of course, scientists who are not concerned over the benefits of their experiments.

We dwell at some length on Swift's attack on science. In broad terms, I divide this issue into two areas: what precisely Swift saw as abuses in science, and how he went about satirizing those abuses. Discussion on the first explores the uses of science, the effect of empirical inquiry on religious beliefs, the implications of the excitement over scientific discoveries on the study of the humanities, and the implications for moral behavior of the excessive pride generated by the new philosophy. For describing the satiric method employed by Swift, I still find Marjorie Nicolson and Nora Mohler's "The Scientific Background of Swift's *Voyage to Laputa*" the most sensible and useful single work. I generally distribute copies of experiments from the *Philosophical Transactions of the Royal Society*, upon which Swift based the experiments at the Grand Academy. I use those experiments as a springboard for providing students with a historical account of seventeenth- and eighteenth-century science as well as to suggest the eclecticism of Swift's genius.

I approach book 4 in a manner suggested by James Clifford's essay "Gulliver's Fourth Voyage: 'Hard' and 'Soft' Schools of Interpretation." I begin by listing several of the basic points of the "hard" school—the Houyhnhnms are a norm or standard for conduct; Swift provides uncompromising standards of behavior to his reader; the ending of the *Travels* is poignant, even tragic—and ask the class to make a theoretical case supporting this view, even if it means playing the devil's advocate. I then list several of the basic tenets of the "soft" school: the Houyhnhnms serve a largely ironic function; Swift does not provide absolute standards; the ending of the *Travels* tends to be comic, with Swift directing laughter at both Gulliver and the reader. With little prompting, students begin to argue over the respective merits of each interpretation. Every point raised by a protagonist of one view receives a rebuttal from a protagonist of the opposing view. There are obvious problems in this schema: it oversimplifies the *Travels* and tends to polarize opinion. These effects are only temporary, however, for the ensuing discussion generally reveals the complexity of the issues in book 4 and extremism tends to fade. This approach, I believe, allows the students to understand the full range of interpretive possibilities, while permitting each to arrive at an individual conclusion through logical argumentation.

This approach also addresses the problems of interpretation presented by the Houyhnhnms. The Yahoos have ceased to be a problem ever since I required my classes to read Roland Frye's "Swift's Yahoo and the Christian Symbols for Sin." This essay allows them to see the Yahoos in the context of a Christian rhetoric for sin and human weakness. It also suggests the necessity of reading Swift in the historical and literary context of his time and the problems encountered when we read him with twentieth-century biases.

Gulliver's Travels lends itself to an interdisciplinary approach, or at least to the use of material from other disciplines. Since both the Yahoos and Swift suffered from the spleen, I discuss medical concepts of melancholia. I describe the ubiquity of melancholy, its psychological and physiological causes, and its relation to creativity and insanity (C. A. Moore's essay "The English Malady," though dated, remains the most informative work on that subject). Our session on melancholy, I have found, provides useful background for reading *The Rape of the Lock*. When we talk about melancholy and insanity, invariably someone raises the question of Swift's mental health, and I take this opportunity to put the insanity issue to rest. In addition to melancholia, we also discuss the myriad of gestures in the *Travels*. I have found the theories of anthropologists such as Desmond Morris and Michael Argyle relevant in establishing the significance of those gestures. The "mimic" and "symbolic" gestures, for instance, in the first two books closely reflect Morris's description of the nonverbal patterns of communication of people placed in an alien culture. I also play a tape recording of Georg Telemann's *Gulliver-Suite*, performed by two of my former graduate students. (When possible I have members of the class perform it, for it is not difficult to learn, can be played on a variety of wind instruments, and does not take long to perform.) Since Telemann's satire is visual as well as aural, I distribute parts of the *Suite* for the class. The first movement, "Lilliputsche Chaconne," consists of diminutive notes (64th and 128th notes); "Brobdingnagische Gigve" consists of whole notes; the attempt of the Laputan servants to awaken their masters from their intellectual reveries by gently tapping is the subject of the third movement, "Reverie der Laputier, nebst ihren Aufweckern." The Houyhnhnms and Yahoos are depicted by the two voices of the final movement. The first voice, "Loure der gesitteten Houyhnhnms," is a logical, well-ordered musical progression; the second, "Furie der unartigen Yahoos," is wildly chaotic. Finally, I show approximately twenty slides I have made from illustrated editions of *Gulliver's Travels*. I use the illustrations of LeFebvre, Grandville, Morten, Brock, Rackham, Lalauze, and Quintanilla, as well as several illustrations from the Classics Illustrated version of the *Travels* (see appendix for bibliographic information).

The class on illustrations is, according to the remarks on students' evaluation forms, the most popular and enjoyable single session we have on *Gulliver's Travels*. Initially, the notion of illustrations prompts them to discuss the visual aspects of Swift's prose. They quickly mention that while reading the *Travels* they had formed mental pictures of people, buildings, and entire episodes. This, in turn, leads them to consider the various elements in Swift's prose—concrete

nouns, clusters of adjectives, appositives, parenthetical statements—
that encourage the reader to do this.

When viewing the illustrations, the students also begin to recognize
that pictures may have a more significant function than merely
supplying decorative ornamentation to a narrative. As they verbalize
the differences between their visualizing of an event and an artist's
rendering of that event, they become aware that illustrations function
as a form of nonverbal criticism, a visual gloss that shapes our
responses. This insight also allows us to explore briefly some attitudes
toward *Gulliver's Travels* and its author in the nineteenth and early
twentieth centuries. By viewing Morten's illustrations of book 4, for
instance, students can see the penchant of the Victorians to conceive
of Swift as a morbid misanthrope: the Yahoos are decidedly human-
looking; English colonizers are seen attacking native women; Pedro de
Mendez's sailors menacingly point guns and a harpoon at Gulliver (this
has no basis in the *Travels*).

By far the most impressive illustrations are the four hundred created
by J. J. Grandville, the nineteenth-century French political cartoonist.
These illustrations are available in a recent edition of *Gulliver's
Travels* (Great Ocean), which I place on a reserve shelf for my class.
Themes and motifs that the students may have missed when reading
the *Travels* now become apparent. Grandville's emphasis on the eyes
of the Brobdingnagians, for instance, prompts them to explore the
significance of the motif of staring or looking intently that appears in
book 2. Since we generally stare at artifacts or freaks of nature and not
at humans, the illustrations help students comprehend the Brobdingnagian conception of Gulliver. Grandville's illustrations of the dispute
between the Big-Endians and the Little-Endians in book 1 and the
operation in the School of Political Projectors, in which the brains of
two disputants are divided in half and exchanged, enter the realm of
fantasy. In the former, the eggs are personified and are engaged in a
mock-heroic struggle using knives and forks. In the latter, two marble
busts of human heads are depicted with a saw cutting through them.
By having the students view these two slides and by asking them to
read several chapters in Eric Rabkin's *The Fantastic in Literature* (also
on reserve), I help them explore Rabkin's notion that "satire is
inherently fantastic" (146).

We can also glimpse changing social mores and changing attitudes
toward *Gulliver's Travels* by examining various illustrations of one
scene. The maids-of-honor episode, for instance, is illustrated by
LeFebvre as a virtual scientific gathering of women, one of whom is
holding a magnifying glass, to examine a wondrous specimen. For C.
E. Brock, courtliness, etiquette, and civility replace sexuality; the

characters are dressed in highly fashionable, oriental-looking clothes with Gulliver kissing the hand of one of the maids. A. D. Lalauze presents a highly erotic scene consisting of seminude women gathered around one of the maids who is rubbing Gulliver between her breasts. The class on illustrations, then, serves, several functions, not the least of which is to suggest to students the diversity of interpretation of *Gulliver's Travels* and the notion that critical interpretation of literary works need not inevitably be verbal.

Gulliver's Travels is one of those rare literary works that have become part of our collective cultural experience. References to it abound in the media, in cartoons, and in the classroom: travel agencies in Phoenix and in York, England, named "Gulliver's Travels"; a motel outside Hamilton, Ontario, named "The Lemuel Gulliver"; a billboard in Columbus, Ohio, reading "Outdoors is Brobdingnagian." Students who have never read the work feel in some way familiar with it. Thus the teacher of *Gulliver's Travels* has an advantage that one rarely experiences in teaching eighteenth-century literature. Students come to us eager to read the work and to learn more about it; they are predisposed to enjoying the *Travels* before they ever read Gulliver's first words. It is up to us not to dampen their enthusiasm or to deflate their expectations but to preserve the wit and excitement and vitality of *Gulliver's Travels*, to make it a living, meaningful work for our students, not simply another fossilized classic.

APPENDIX

LeFebvre's illustrations originally appeared in a limited edition, *Voyages de Gulliver*, published in Paris in 1797. His illustrations appear in Lenfest, "LeFebvre's Illustrations." Jean Ignace Isidore Gerard Grandville's illustrations appear in *Gulliver's Travels* (Arlington: Great Ocean, 1980); Thomas Morten's in *Gulliver's Travels* (London; 1865); C. E. Brock's in *Gulliver's Travels* (London, 1894) and (selected) in the Signet paperback edition (New York, 1960); Arthur Rackham's in *Gulliver's Travels* (London: Dent; New York: Dutton, 1909); A. D. Lalauze's in *Gulliver's Travels* (Paris, 1875); and Luis Quintanilla's in *Gulliver's Travels* (New York: Crown, 1947). The Classics Illustrated version of *Gulliver's Travels* appears in issue no. 16 of that series (New York: Gilberton, 1946). Several illustrations of most of the artists I have cited above, as well as the work of numerous other illustrators, appear in Swift, *The Annotated* Gulliver's Travels. If you wish to examine a wide variety of illustrations, see Lenfest, "Checklist."

Introducing Swift's Satiric Themes and Techniques: *Gulliver's Travels*, Part 2, Chapter 7

Sidney Gottlieb

Like many others, I introduce *Gulliver's Travels* in my undergraduate survey course in Restoration and eighteenth-century literature by first assigning *A Modest Proposal* and *The Battle of the Books*. *A Modest Proposal*, as teachers through the years have confirmed, provides perhaps the best first step toward understanding certain characteristics of Swift's satiric technique, particularly the use of a veiled persona whose accelerating enthusiasm clashes with his pretense of "reasonableness." *The Battle of the Books*, though also interesting in terms of style, serves the somewhat different purpose in my class of introducing a remarkably complete list of Swift's recurrent satiric targets and themes, clustered around dramatizations of the innumerable perversities of the Moderns. To make a coherent transition from these works to *Gulliver's Travels*, I spend class time on a close reading of a brief but highly significant episode in part 2, chapter 7, that synthesizes the stylistic subtlety of *A Modest Proposal* and the thematic background of *The Battle of the Books*: Gulliver's speech to the king of Brobdingnag in praise of gunpowder.

It is helpful to set the scene quickly in its dramatic context: Gulliver has just given a lengthy panegyric upon his home country, only to be devastatingly cross-examined by the king, who concludes that Gulliver and his fellow Englishmen must be "the most pernicious Race of little odious Vermin that Nature ever suffered to crawl upon the Surface of the Earth" (*Writings* 108). To demonstrate the king's *"Narrowness of Thinking"* (109) and restore the dignity of humankind, Gulliver fires his best shot, ironically one that blows up in his own face. The relevant section can be read aloud in class and is quoted here in full:

> In hopes to ingratiate my self farther into his Majesty's Favour, I told him of an Invention discovered between three and four hundred Years ago, to make a certain Powder; into an heap of which the smallest Spark of Fire falling, would kindle the whole in a Moment, although it were as big as a Mountain; and make it all fly up in the Air together, with a Noise and Agitation greater than Thunder. That, a proper Quantity of this Powder rammed into an hollow Tube of Brass or Iron, according to its Bigness, would drive a Ball of Iron or Lead with such Violence and Speed, as nothing was able to sustain its Force. That, the largest Balls

thus discharged, would not only Destroy whole Ranks of an Army
at once; but batter the strongest Walls to the Ground; sink down
Ships with a thousand Men in each, to the Bottom of the Sea; and
when linked together by a Chain, would cut through Masts and
Rigging; divide Hundreds of Bodies in the Middle, and lay all
Waste before them. That we often put this Powder into large
hollow Balls of Iron, and discharged them by an Engine into some
City we were besieging; which would rip up the Pavement, tear
the Houses to Pieces, burst and throw Splinters on every Side,
dashing out the Brains of all who came near. That I knew the
Ingredients very well, which were Cheap, and common; I
understood the Manner of compounding them, and could direct
his Workmen how to make those Tubes of a Size proportionable
to all other Things in his Majesty's Kingdom; and the largest need
not be above two hundred Foot long; twenty or thirty of which
Tubes, charged with the proper Quantity of Powder and Balls,
would batter down the Walls of the strongest Town in his
Dominions in a few Hours; or destroy the whole Metropolis, if
ever it should pretend to dispute his absolute Commands. This I
humbly offered to his Majesty, as a small Tribute of Acknowledg-
ment in return of so many Marks that I had received of his Royal
Favour and Protection.

The King was struck with Horror at the Description I had given
of those terrible Engines, and the Proposal I had made. . . . (109-
10)

By the end of this section we hardly need the king's commentary to
appreciate how ridiculous and dangerous Gulliver's proposal is. Few
readers, even in an introductory course, miss Swift's basic point that
any argument for human dignity and intelligence is weakened, not
strengthened, by reference to inventions designed to kill. But although
the general meaning of this passage is largely self-explanatory and
clear, a close analytical rereading helps dramatize the various subtleties that make it a rhetorical and thematic tour de force. We certainly
feel the power of Swift's prose at the end but need to go back clause by
clause to see how the passage accelerates: from innocence to experience, from charming curiosity to cynical tyranny, from vagueness to
quantifiable precision, from wonder to horror. I try not to introduce
these terms before the discussion: students have a remarkable way of
seeing things just as teachers want them to if we set up strict
interpretive parameters. Rather, these terms or ones like them should
emerge inductively, though perhaps with occasional bits of prodding
and direction, from the collaborative reading in class. What follows in

the next paragraphs, then, is perhaps best taken not as the stuff of a lecture but as an indication of what a good class discussion can generate.

When we go back to the first sentence after reading the entire passage, it is particularly easy to see that Gulliver at least begins tamely and inoffensively. Using the technique of delayed decoding, to borrow a useful term from Ian Watt (174-80), he purposely avoids mentioning the word *gunpowder* directly and instead describes a spectacular scene through sensory details that seem mysterious and suspenseful, as though we are witnessing the effects of this "certain Powder" for the first time. From this innocent, even childlike perspective the explosion is spontaneous, magical, and thoroughly fascinating.

By the next sentence, though, this perspective changes subtly but noticeably. Students are usually quick to see that Gulliver now describes a human intervention into what was initially a natural wonder, and it takes little prodding to come up with examples of how this sentence moves us from a world of magic to a somewhat more ominous world of technology. Gulliver still uses naive description—"an hollow Tube of Brass or Iron" rather than "cannon," for example—but he shows a new concern for scientific measurement and exactitude: even the mere mention of weighing out "a proper Quantity of this Powder" is suspicious, especially to readers who have just come from Swift's unforgettable satire on the quantifying mentality, *A Modest Proposal*. Equally ominous is the way in which the powder is now under human control, no longer set off by "the smallest Spark of Fire falling" from some indeterminate place, but purposefully "rammed" into a hollow tube that is presumably made, not found. The force of this explosion is now not so much charming as it is awe-inspiring.

The tone changes even more markedly in the next sentence, in part because the setting shifts: instead of exploding impressively but harmlessly in some indefinite space, the cannon balls are discharged in places occupied by a great many human beings—"whole Ranks . . . a thousand . . . Hundreds." As in *A Modest Proposal*, for Swift the purest form of a statistic is a body count, and there are bodies galore in Gulliver's chillingly impersonal description of increasing destruction. Note in particular the curious phrasing when Gulliver tells that "the largest Balls . . . would not only Destroy whole Ranks of an Army at once; but batter the strongest Walls to the Ground," as if the latter were of far more consequence than the former. Alongside this impersonality is a growing excitement, evident in the piling of clause upon clause in this long sentence. (Reading this part out loud will convey how effectively Swift embeds the excitement in the style.)

Gulliver gives as many examples as he can to illustrate his theme, but they become more and more horrifying, not more impressive: the cannon balls not only kill people but mangle the bodies, and the vision at the close of this sentence is of extensive, if not universal, "Waste."

Gulliver's enthusiasm, always a suspicious quality in Swift's work, is on full display from here to the end of the speech. Perhaps most noticeably, in the next sentence he continues to be fascinated by gruesome details. If in the previous sentence, giving him the benefit of our doubts, he seems to speak like a general about what is at least arguably the military usefulness of gunpowder, he now speaks more like a madman about "dashing out the Brains of all who came near." This sentence is even more rapid and excited than the previous one, concluding with a series of short phrases connected by commas, not semicolons. Now more and more attuned to subtleties in this passage, students may notice even further significant details. For example, whereas the structure of previous sentences is often conditional or passive (e.g., "the largest Balls thus discharged, would . . . Destroy . . . "), Gulliver speaks here in the active voice, and the events he describes are not hypothetical but real and habitual: " . . . we often put this Powder into large hollow Balls of Iron, and discharged them by an Engine into some City we were besieging." Interestingly, for the first time in the narrative part of the speech Gulliver begins to use first-person pronouns, plural here and singular in the next sentence: this works to erode even the appearance of objectivity and introduces the theme that dominates the climax of this episode, Gulliver's self-serving, arrogant pride.

As we reach the conclusion of this scene, which Swift has carefully accelerated, the ironies become less and less subtle. The following sentence, the longest in the passage, hits almost literally with the power of a two-hundred-foot-long cannon. Students are quick to point out that when Gulliver tries to adapt human weaponry to a Brobding-nagian scale he envisions a kind of doomsday device that rightly provokes outrage rather than gratitude and satirizes rather than glorifies its advocate. This weapon is frightening not only because of its size but because of the way Gulliver aims it, at least in his imagination, at the land of his benevolent host. Not the least of Gulliver's many mistakes is that he completely misunderstands the person to whom he offers new technological power: the king is pained, not pleased, by Gulliver's fantasy of the destruction of his "whole Metropolis." But the most deeply disturbing revelation comes at the final moment of Gulliver's narration, as he triumphantly proclaims that gunpowder serves a ruler well by helping him obliterate any who would "dispute his absolute Commands." This completes Swift's quick history of science, dramatizing his view that it may begin in delight and wonder but ends inevitably in cataclysmic destruction and tyranny. It is no surprise that the king—as well as most modern readers—responds to Gulliver's modest proposal, however "humbly offered," with horror.

A fully developed analysis of this episode needs at least some awareness of the broader extratextual backgrounds on which Swift relies. He no doubt expected his eighteenth-century readers to recognize a few key allusions in this scene, and it may be worth trying to integrate this material into class discussion. Generally speaking, Gulliver's argument instantly identifies him as a Modern by recalling the familiar claim, echoed throughout much of the contemporary scientific and philosophical literature, that the invention of the mariner's compass, the printing press, and gunpowder confirms the superiority of the Moderns over the Ancients. At the same time, Gulliver's confident claim is thoroughly undermined by repeated allusions to book 6 of *Paradise Lost*. Even before the king of Brobdingnag protests that "some evil Genius, Enemy to Mankind, must have been the first Contriver" (110) of explosive devices, it is clear that Satan's speech on the invention of gunpowder and cannon for use in the battle against the loyal angels in heaven (esp. 6.469-95) is the rhetorical and thematic model for Gulliver.

But while I feel that such background material is important and that, for example, a detailed comparison of the speeches of Satan and Gulliver would elicit a fascinating discussion or written assignment in an advanced class on Swift, in an introductory survey class I find it most helpful at least to begin with the kind of close reading approach I describe herein. Extensive discussion of this key episode serves a number of useful purposes. At the very least, it helps make a transition from our study of Swift's earlier satiric works to our study of *Gulliver's Travels*, and it prepares the class for part 3, which obviously expands on the critique of science and technology, and part 4, where Gulliver is again the focal point of the satire. But even more important, I use such a discussion to demonstrate how carefully Swift, at his best, uses his style not so much to relate as to embody and dramatize the key ideas of *Gulliver's Travels*. Perhaps teachers no longer have to anticipate disparaging comments on Swift's style, such as Samuel Johnson's celebrated remark that "When once you have thought of big men and little men, it is very easy to do all the rest" (Boswell 2: 319). But I believe that we must show our students in class how accessible Swift's work can be and that a close examination of his style is a remarkably effective way to understand and feel the power of *Gulliver's Travels*.

Teaching the Third Voyage

Michael DePorte

From the beginning book 3 has been the ugly duckling of the *Travels*. Not even Swift's Scriblerian friends were very fond of this most Scriblerian of Gulliver's voyages: Arbuthnot called it the "least Brilliant"; Gay, the "least entertaining" (*Correspondence* 3: 179, 183). In the nineteenth century, Jeffrey assured readers of the *Edinburgh Review* that the third voyage, besides being dull, exposed Swift's absolute "incapacity for large and comprehensive views," while Coleridge said he would "expunge" it entirely as "a wretched abortion, the product of spleen and ignorance and self conceit" (Williams, *Critical Heritage* 320, 334). This disregard persists in the twentieth century: William A. Eddy judges it "at once the longest and the worst" (157); Ricardo Quintana speaks of its "marked inferiority" (*Mind and Art* 315); and Marjorie Nicolson and Nora M. Mohler, whose research challenged many assumptions about the book, do not really challenge the traditional assessment of its literary quality.

Though in recent years a number of studies devoted to the merits of book 3 have appeared (see Sutherland, Munro, Traldi, and especially Mezciems), most of us, I suspect, still find it tricky to teach. It lacks the quality of primal fantasy so evident in the other three books: the fantasy of power in book 1, of impotence in book 2, of wise aliens in book 4. It is the voyage that least invites novelistic readings. Gulliver's role is almost exclusively that of observer: he sees much but has far less to say or do than in Lilliput or Brobdingnag. No compelling narrative line connects the various episodes together—what, after all, has the flying island to do with Struldbruggs or apparitions of the dead? And the trip home, in which "nothing happen[s] worth mentioning," seems altogether perfunctory. It is, moreover, the most referential of the four books. Allusions—topical, historical, literary, scientific, and philosophical—intrude everywhere. To pursue them rigorously is to risk losing one's class in the thickets of explanation; to ignore them altogether may leave students with the impression that Swift's ridicule of science and technology, however hilarious, is sophomoric and ill-informed. And with or without explanation, the jibes at the Dutch that frame the voyage are apt to strike modern ears as unpleasantly jingoistic.

I see little point in straining one's ingenuity (and one's students' capacity for belief) to prove that everything in book 3 works like a charm and that what is not conspicuously brilliant must be covertly so. The attacks on the Dutch *are* heavy-handed; the ending *does* disappoint; as adventures the various episodes *are* less engaging. But I think a strong case can be made in the classroom for the satiric power of these episodes, for the artful way in which they are connected, and for their importance to the design of the *Travels*. Much of this case will emerge from discussion if students are asked certain questions: Could one scramble the order of the episodes without changing the effect of the book? Would our response to the book differ were Gulliver to confront Struldbruggs at the beginning? Why might Swift wish to follow the account of scientists and engineers with a magical visitation of ghosts? Just how does this presentation of the past play off against the way men contemplate the future in Laputa and Lagado? And so on.

Book 3 may lack the immediate power of the other books, but it has a delayed power derived in some measure from its narrative defects: because the connections between parts are not always clear we must work them out, and we cannot work them out unless we consider fully what they mean.

The name of Gulliver's third unlucky ship, the *Hopewell*, provides a significant clue to the concerns that underlie this voyage. Whether we take it as a sardonic injunction (hope well!) or as a reference to psychic terrain (the well of hope), the name suggests that book 3 is about hope, or rather, about hope running dry. For each of the lands Gulliver visits turns out to be a land of false promise. Book 3 is Swift's satire on wishful thinking.

Let us examine hope first in its utopian aspect. Laputa and Lagado explode the sentimental view of science and technology as tickets to future utopias. The flying island is a material success. Control of flight has given the islanders security from invasion and domination of the mainland below. They live, Gulliver says, surrounded by "Plenty and Magnificence" on the "the most delicious Spot of Ground in the World" (Davis ed. 149). But their privileged position brings them no joy; worship of science has poisoned every aspect of Laputan life. The astronomers exhaust themselves in speculation, the chief fruit of which is a terror of cosmic disaster that keeps them awake nights. In their obsession with the future they have lost the most precious of the future's gifts: hope. They drag along in a stupor of anxiety, unable to take pleasure in friends and family, let alone in the bounty around them. Marriage in Laputa is an unrelieved catastrophe. The astronomers are such miserable companions that their wives run off at the earliest opportunity; any other life is preferable. Recently, the wife of the prime minister forsook the luxuries of her position to dwell in squalor on the mainland with an old, deformed footman who beat her daily.

The calamities of the Laputans are largely psychological; those of their disciples at Lagado largely physical. The projectors are hopeful enough, but the countryside is in ruins, the people starving, and they themselves no closer to their goals than when they began. The grand old projector of the academy, *"the universal Artist,"* who for thirty years has devoted himself to "the Improvement of human Life," has such passion for his projects that he never considers how naked sheep or solidified air will benefit humankind should he succeed in producing them (166). The only projects that do not seem crackbrained are those that steer clear of technology and seek to advance society by intelligent application of what is known already about human nature: treat statesmen for physical and mental diseases that may affect their conduct of office; tax individuals on their vices or, better yet, on the qualities (generally vices as well) they esteem in themselves; choose public officials for their wisdom and virtue. Note the trap Swift lays here for napping readers by embedding sane ideas amid crazy ones and by having Gulliver call the proposal for virtuous government the looniest he ever heard of. As always, inconsistency is crucial to Swift's satire. We cannot assume that because every project at Lagado thus far has been nutty all of them will be, nor that because Gulliver's responses in Laputa and Lagado have thus far been sensible they will continue to make sense. The promise of high science and applied technology is heady: to cut loose from the past and soar into new regions of possibility. What Lagado and Laputa in fact offer is a choice between fake hope and foolish despair.

Gulliver's encounter with the dead in Glubbdubdrib addresses the antithetical but equally sentimental desire to embrace the past as mother of all excellence. On casual reading, the revelations of the departed appear to support just this view of history. When asked to assess the rival theories of Gassendi and Descartes, Aristotle magisterially dismisses them both. When Gulliver summons the senate of Rome to present itself alongside a modern legislature, the one impresses him as an "assembly of Heroes and Demy-Gods," the other as a "Knot of Pedlars, Pick-pockets, Highwaymen and Bullies" (180). Looking back on the revelations of the dead, Gulliver reports that he "was chiefly disgusted with modern History" (183). But if the Ancients generally come across better than the Moderns we must not forget that Sir Thomas More is listed in the *"Sextumvirate"* of incomparable worthies and that a good deal of what Gulliver picks up from the dead is uncongenial to idealized visions of antiquity. Alexander the Great confides that he died a drunkard, Caesar that Brutus did the world a favor by stabbing him. The one unrewarded patriot whose story Gulliver chooses to tell lived in Rome's golden age and was slighted by Augustus himself. For Swift, utopia is no more a province of long ago than a province of the future. He may share with lovers of the past the view that progress is a desperate, tawdry illusion, but he wants no part of their consolation. To muse on the perfections of a golden age while accepting decay as inevitable is to school oneself to compliance: what one cannot fight, one need not fight.

The satire on pipe dreams reaches its culmination with the account of the Struldbruggs. Here Swift confronts humanity's deepest longing—to elude death—and he prepares the ground with care. When Gulliver learns that there are people in Luggnagg who live forever he cannot contain himself; he bursts into raptures at the thought of men living free of the "Weight and Depression of Spirits caused by the continual Apprehension of Death" (192) and eagerly outlines what he would do with immortality: First, he would amass wealth. With careful investments he should have no trouble becoming the richest man in the kingdom after a few hundred years. Next, he would acquire learning. By pursuing a diligent program of reading and keeping a detailed political and cultural record of passing times he would eventually know more than anyone else in the kingdom, at which point he and like-minded Struldbruggs might form a council to advise humankind. It is the chance to benefit society that fires Gulliver's imagination. The instruction and example of these godlike beings would, Gulliver says, "probably prevent that continual Degeneracy of human Nature, so justly complained of in all Ages." On top of all this, he could have the satisfaction of seeing "great Inventions brought to the utmost Perfection"—the discovery of perpetual motion, for instance, or of the "universal Medicine" (194).

As a Struldbrugg, Gulliver believes, he would have everything to hope for. In reality, of course, he would have nothing to hope for. So far are Struldbruggs from escaping the "Depression of Spirits" attendant upon ordinary life that at thirty they sink into a depression from which they never emerge. For it is then Struldbruggs begin to contemplate what fate has in store: loss of health, loss of friends, loss of status, loss of reason and memory, an eternity of Alzheimer's disease. After seeing a few Struldbruggs Gulliver is "heartily ashamed of the pleasing Visions" he formed of immortality and swears that "no Tyrant could invent a Death into which [he] would not run with Pleasure from such a Life" (198). The Struldbruggs are, significantly, the last exotic people Gulliver meets before his voyage to Houyhnhnmland. They afford a peculiarly horrifying demonstration of the point Swift makes throughout book 3: dreams of perfectibility, whether vested in utopias of the future or golden ages of the past, are just that—dreams. The human condition is hostile to perfection. The Struldbruggs prepare us for what is to come: anything perfect must, by implication, be other than human.

This brings us to consider the place book 3 occupies in the plan of the *Travels*, an issue best approached by reminding students that book 3 was written last. More often than not this fact has been used to explain the apparent miscellaneousness of the voyage, the apparent dispersion of energy. Swift, the argument runs, had various secondary targets he had not gotten around to attacking. Having reached the climax of his satire in book 4, he could relax and lark about on lesser hobbyhorses (see, for example Quintana, *Mind and Art* 315-16 and *Swift* 161; Dobrée 455-56).

But there is another, more interesting explanation. Swift may have written book 3 because he felt something important was missing. Perhaps he feared book 4 might be taken to burlesque the life of reason and added his new book to furnish unmistakable examples of reason run amok. And though "soft" readings of the fourth book hardly support such speculation, we should remember that until the last fifty years no one viewed the Houyhnhnms as possible targets of satire and that arguments to prove them targets typically require a good deal of finesse. Without book 3 it would surely be easier to maintain that wholly rational societies like that of the Houyhnhnms are meant to seem ludicrous and unpleasant.

As it stands, the contrast with the Laputans shows the difference between true reason and false. Dissension among Houyhnhnms is unknown because among them reason is true reason, and true reason will always lead those who employ it to the same conclusions. The Laputans, however, are "vehemently given to Opposition"; they dispute "every Inch of a Party Opinion" and are keenest when, as is commonly the case, they know nothing whatever of the matter (147-48). Indeed, it is the Laputans, not the Houyhnhnms, who are narrowly rational. In poetry, Gulliver says, Houyhnhnms "must be allowed to excel all other Mortals" (257); Laputans are such complete strangers to "Imagination, Fancy, and Invention" that they do not even have words for them in their language. As we have seen, high science betrays the Laputans into a nightmare of tedium and neurotic dread. It also opens a back door to superstition: on the sly, they cast horoscopes. Unlike Houyhnhnms, who value friendship and society, Laputans reject the claims of feeling altogether. They aspire to a purely mental existence, and their passions, denied legitimate outlets, exact an appropriate revenge.

The abuse of reason, obvious in the preoccupations of the Laputans and experiments of the projectors, is also a recurring motif in Gulliver's meeting with the shades: misguided commentators on Homer and Aristotle, kings who contend "with great Strength of Reason" that corruption is essential to government, philosophers who reduce the mysteries of nature to logical systems.

The recurrent lesson of book 3, that a life of pure reason lies beyond human endeavor, is central to the meaning of the *Travels*. It is also preeminent among the many lessons Gulliver fails to learn. He becomes at the end a martyr to wishful thinking. The letter to his cousin Sympson leaves no doubt that the Gulliver who as a youth had "been a Sort of Projector" (162), has embarked on a project worthy of Lagado. There is nothing wrong with getting spiders to spin colored silk, bottling sunbeams against cloudy days, or confecting delicacies from excrement, except that such enterprises fail. Nor is anything wrong in trying to make Houyhnhnms of men save the hopelessness of it, which drives one mad.

"In what ordure hast thou dipped thy pencil?": Problems in Teaching Part 4

Brian Corman

Few fictional tales—and fewer classic tales—have provoked more consistently hostile response than "A Voyage to the Country of the Houyhnhnms." Its seventy-four pages (in the Davis edition) have offended readers of many sorts for over 250 years. A few brief, well-known passages exhibit the nature and persistence of these reactions:

> In this last part of his imaginary travels, Swift has indulged a misanthropy that is intolerable. The representation which he has given us of human nature, must terrify, and even debase the reader who views it. . . . In painting the Yahoos he becomes one himself. (John Boyle, fifth Earl of Orrery, 1752; Williams, *Critical Heritage* 126-27)

> Misanthropy is so dangerous a thing, and goes so far in sapping the very foundation of morality and religion, that I esteem the last part of Swift's *Gulliver* (that I mean relative to his Houyhnhnms and Yahoos) to be a worse book to peruse than those which we forbid as the most flagitious and obscene. (James Harris, 1781; Donoghue 93)

> The meanness of Swift's nature, and his rigid incapacity for dealing with the grandeurs of the human spirit, with religion, with poetry or even with science when it rose above the mercenary practical, is absolutely appalling. His own Yahoo is not a more abominable one-sided degradation of humanity than is he himself. (Thomas De Quincey, 1847; Donoghue 116)

> Some of this audience mayn't have read the last part of *Gulliver*, and to such I would recall the advice of the venerable Mr. Punch to persons about to marry, and say, 'Don't'. . . : a monster gibbering shrieks, and gnashing imprecations against mankind—tearing down all shreds of modesty, past all sense of manliness and shame; filthy in word, filthy in thought, furious, raging, obscene. . . . (William Makepeace Thackeray, 1851; Donoghue 116-17)

> Among the Houyhnhnms probability is ruthlessly sacrificed to the wild pleasure the author takes in trampling human pride in the mire of his sarcasm. Of the horrible foulness of this satire on

the Yahoos enough will have been said when it is admitted that it banishes from decent households a fourth part of one of the most brilliant and delightful of English books.   (Edmund Gosse, 1889; 161-62)

We have, then, in his writings probably the most remarkable expression of negative feelings and attitudes that literature can offer—the spectacle of creative powers (the paradoxical description seems right) exhibited consistently in negation and rejection.   (F. R. Leavis, 1952; 86)

Swift has had as many defenders as antagonists, of course, from John Hawkesworth and John Wesley to R. S. Crane and C. J. Rawson. But the hostile responses sampled above are never vanquished by the enlightened explanations of the many readers who have responded (in my view) with superior sympathy and/or understanding, and it is with these ever-present rejecters of Swift that the teacher of part 4 must contend.

In his oft-quoted letter to Pope (29 Sept. 1725), Swift proclaimed that "the chief end I propose myself in all my labours is to vex the world rather than divert it" (*Correspondence* 3: 103). Few writers have been more successful in their stated goals. The *Travels* (and part 4 in particular) is a unique mixture of comedy, irony, and satire, working sometimes in harmony, other times not, to address the most fundamental questions about human nature. There is little agreement about the precise workings of the comic, the ironic, and the satiric elements and perhaps still less about the significance of many specific details and incidents. Most readers, however, regardless of persuasion, echo John Hawkesworth's view that Swift's general design is "to mortify pride, which . . . produces not only the most ridiculous follies, but the most extensive calamity" (Williams, *Critical Heritage* 154). There is also much agreement about the vehicle, since most readers begin with Swift's own explanation in the same letter to Pope, in which he speaks of loving individuals but hating "that animal called man" and of erecting his "Travells" on a definition of humankind as "*rationis capax*" rather than "*animal rationale*" (3: 103). Swift's comments can and have been interpreted in many ways, but in pointing to the issues that most concerned him in writing the *Travels*, he points also to the issues that have troubled its readers ever since. Irvin Ehrenpreis's recent summary of the general impact of Swift's masterpiece on its readers seems incontrovertible: "we feel drawn into a radical, comical criticism of human nature which leaves us unsure of our axioms, offers no clear set of rules to replace them, and challenges us to reconsider our instinctive patterns of life" (*Swift* 3: 455).

Generations of readers have of course been diverted by the *Travels*, despite Swift's stated intentions, though often in abridged versions and frequently without part 4 entirely. But generations of readers—often the same readers who are diverted—have also been vexed. To be unsettled about something as fundamental as human nature is not the goal of most readers. And when Swift refuses to offer solace for lost illusions, his readers, students, and even their teachers, often rebel. Because Swift's argument is so basic and so powerful, the most frequent such response is evasion. Traditionally, this evasion takes throo forms: (1) the formal or moral dismissal· any writers (forms) unable to offer a life-affirming answer to the problems they pose are unworthy of our serious concern; (2) the ad hominem dismissal: Swift was a demented misanthropist and therefore unworthy of our serious concern; and (3) the apology: if you read carefully you will see that Swift is not really trying to vex us.

All three evasions (though the first two more frequently) are to be found in the Swift criticism, often in highly influential books and articles. They are also found in many students who first encounter Swift in the university courses we teach. Their language and arguments are rarely as sophisticated, but the strategies remain the same, on either side of the desk, because the problem is the same: What can be done to undermine the force of Swift's presentation of the human condition in part 4?

The first two responses, often preconditioned, are only exacerbated by Swift's treatment of his reader. We expect satire to be general, assaults on pride to be aimed at all of humankind. We are rarely made uncomfortable by, say, Pope's generalized attack on pride in *An Essay on Man*; granting Pope his argument is an intellectual exercise and nothing more. But, as Claude Rawson has shown, Swift's method in the *Travels* is quite different. The angry assault is Gulliver's, but it "reflect[s] a cooler needling offensiveness from the Swift who manipulates the 'switch.'" The voice is not Swift's, "but there is really no sufficiently vivid alternative point of view that we can hang on to at the final moment." The reader is never let off the hook as part 4 progresses from "a needling defiance and the openly unfriendly intimacy of a petty insult" to a "quarrelsome hysteria." Although "the hysteria is Gulliver's, . . . the quarrel with the reader is one which Swift has been conducting through Gulliver" (Rawson, *Gulliver* 12).

Having been made to feel that his attack is personal, most readers are predisposed to resist whatever conclusions he offers. But Swift's principal conclusion is difficult to resist, in that (in its most reduced form) it is hardly more than a restatement that we are proud and should be less so, something most of us have heard before and many of us believe. (Several critics have demonstrated that Swift's view of pride is a thoroughly conventional position for an Anglican priest.) It is the medium, then, and not the message, that offends, and it is against the medium that resistance is often directed. But here, again, there are difficulties for the resisting reader. Swift is not Gulliver; this has become perhaps the central commonplace for teachers of the *Travels*. We often forget that recognizing this essential fact does little to solve our problems as readers. We know what Gulliver thinks; he presents his conclusions in no uncertain terms. But what beyond a traditional attack on pride is in Swift's mind? We sense that we don't like it, but our uncertainty about it remains, producing a more powerful because unfocused discomfort. And this discomfort is only reinforced by Swift's brilliant irony. (Swift remains, I believe, the first and unanimous choice for textbooks of irony in English.)

Nor does additional study of Swift's irony offer much relief. The best studies merely confirm our initial suspicions that Swift uses irony in many ways, often simultaneously, to treat complex issues complexly. Swift's irony rarely cuts but one way. If the Yahoos are its target, we expect the Houyhnhnms and/or Gulliver to offer a corrective alternative. Since often they do, our expectations are encouraged. But sometimes they do not, and occasionally the Houyhnhnms themselves become Swift's target. After Swift's irony establishes and then undercuts our expectations repeatedly, we tend to object. Satirists are supposed to offer correctives to the vices they uncover. "The poet is bound, and that *ex officio*, to give his reader some one precept of moral virtue, and to caution him against some one particular vice or folly" (Dryden 2: 146). Satirists are supposed to be committed moralists by profession. Although great satire derives its greatness from the power of its attack, we expect a solution to follow the presentation of the problem. Swift does not, of course, always refuse to meet our expectations. The more localized and particular his attack, the more likely he is to provide a solution. *The Drapier's Letters* offers an obvious, comfortable example, and even the far more disturbing *Modest Proposal* affords considerable reassurance to those who look for answers. Such reassurance, however, is almost entirely absent from part 4. (Recent critics who see the Houyhnhnms as deists or the Yahoos as oppressed Irish colonials seem to be attempting to localize the satire in part 4 in order to minimize its force.) "Whereas in ordinary satires the attack is on a third person for the sake of the reader's pleasure, in this satire the second and third persons of the usual satiric triangle are merged, since the attack is on that general human nature with which the reader is unavoidably identified" (Rader 256). It is no wonder that readers (and teachers) of part 4 cry foul. The danger, however, is in allowing our desire for the comfort of positive alternatives to sanction easy ways out, moral or formal, of the discomfiting outrage provoked by Swift's attack.

Invoking a critical standard or moral principle that requires satire or the satirist to balance objection with affirmation would be one way to allay our outrage. An analogous way is to question the motives of the satirist who seems so intent on destroying, so little interested in rebuilding. A wide range of explanations, from a lack of Christian charity to an "excremental vision," has been offered, and they are often interesting explorations of the unusual mind of Jonathan Swift. At its best, such analysis helps explain the force of Swift's indignation: it is quite possible, for example, that "Swift's mode of assailing pride is possible only to one who, indeed, recognizes an 'excremental vision'" (Rosenheim, *Swift* 232). The danger in such psychological analysis, like the danger in formal and moral analysis, is not in its treatment of Swift but in its tendency to offer the easy alternative to confronting the substance of Swift's attack in part 4. If Swift is wicked or neurotic, he can be condemned or ignored. This, again, seems to me the wrong answer. We need not, finally, accept Swift's pessimistic vision of the human condition, but we must reject that vision rather than its author or its form. However unpleasant or unbalanced we find Swift the man, however distasteful we find satire as a form, we are not justified in dismissing part 4 on either ground alone.

Perhaps the most insidious form of evasion is the third, a product almost exclusively of twentieth-century critics. The critic here tries to offer solace by showing that the outrage we feel is really unintentional on Swift's part and indeed is the result of misreading. (Nineteenth-century critics were able to realize such views through expurgation, particularly in versions prepared for children.) The complexity of Swift's satire offers such critics considerable ammunition, as they build their counteroffensive on any of the following observations: (1) the Yahoos are not only thoroughly repugnant but so devoid of soul and reason that they cannot possibly represent us; (2) the Houyhnhnms are similarly soulless in their adherence to reason alone; (3) Captain Pedro de Mendez is a truly good man, a model for what we all can achieve; (4) Gulliver's ludicrous misanthropy at the end reveals a madman whose views are not to be taken seriously. All these observations are probably accurate, though each has been and continues to be disputed. But problems arise when they are offered in aid of large, comforting conclusions.

Since they lack reason entirely, the Yahoos lead a life devoted to satisfying the desires of their passions. But there should be little solace in our dissimilarities, since we are nonetheless often worse. Similarly, the Houyhnhnms fall short of most human models of perfection: we find their coldness chilling and their chauvinism ridiculous. But their failure to live up to our ideals does not bring us any closer to those same ideals. It follows, then, that the many attempts to use the Houyhnhnms and Yahoos as polar opposites in a dialectic constructed to lead us to a golden mean (typical terms of such dialectics are reason and passion, innocence and experience, or superego and id) make a virtue of that middle state which for Swift is merely a necessity.

The presence of Captain Mendez does hasten the process of distancing us from Gulliver that begins with his departure from the Houyhnhnms. Gulliver has been discomposed so thoroughly by his experiences among them that even a good man is unable to offer him much comfort. When we see his fully developed misanthropy and its resultant reclusive behavior, we tend to reject Gulliver—but that rejection does not negate the cause of his misanthropy. Neither the captain's goodness nor Gulliver's ludicrous despair makes us or our condition any better. The most difficult task, then, for the teacher of part 4 is to disallow these various attempts at evasion or consolation in favor of direct confrontation of the powerful and disturbing vision Swift creates in the final voyage of *Gulliver's Travels*.

Sexuality and the Body

Christopher Fox

What does a student, reading the *Travels* for the first time, do with those Brobdingnagian breasts? or with that "frolicksome" maid of honor who uses Gulliver as a sexual plaything? with Gulliver's defense of his innocence in an affair with a Lilliputian lady, or his account of those Laputan wives who are "exceedingly fond" of strangers arriving "from . . . below"? with Gulliver's naked encounter with the Yahoo maiden, or his closing rejection of his own wife? Whatever the response, it will not be simple. In the classroom, as in criticism, Swift's treatment of sexuality tends to evoke a wide range of responses, from absolute shock to befuddled amusement. Nonetheless, a teacher might be able to guide them to get at some broader questions in the book.

As a theme, sexuality is of course not unique to *Gulliver*; it appears elsewhere in Swift—in "The Lady's Dressing Room," for example, where Strephon takes a tour of Caelia's toilette after she has emerged as a beautiful woman. Strephon is destroyed by what he discovers and, thereafter, we are told,

> His foul Imagination links
> Each Dame he sees with all her Stinks:
> And, if unsav'ry Odours fly,
> Conceives a Lady standing by. (*Poems* 2: 529)

This parallels Gulliver's experience with a series of women in the *Travels*: the dressing rooms of the Brobdingnagian maids, for instance, where he is repulsed by the "very offensive Smell" that "came from their Skins" (Davis ed. 118); his report of a female Yahoo's cruising for young males, "at which time it was observed, that she had a most *offensive Smell*" (264); or his total revulsion from his own wife, whose "very Smell," he finds at the end of book 4, to be "intolerable" (289). (And this, after leaving her "big with Child" at the beginning of the same book.) Can we say then that Gulliver, like Strephon, links "each Dame he sees with all her Stinks"? Students might find other parallels. Like Strephon, Gulliver has not only a nose but an eye for the ugly, particularly when it comes to women. In book 2, for instance, Gulliver notes that the maids of honor

> would strip themselves to the Skin . . . while I was placed on their
> Toylet directly before their naked Bodies; which, I am sure, to
> me was very far from a tempting Sight. . . . Their Skins appeared
> so coarse and uneven . . . with a Mole here and there as broad as a

Trencher, and Hairs hanging from it thicker than Pack-threads; to say nothing further concerning the rest of their Persons. (119)

To this visually shocking detail, Gulliver adds the following, again inviting the reader to guess the rest:

Neither did they at all scruple while I was by, to discharge what they had drunk . . . in a Vessel that held above three Tuns. The handsomest among these Maids of Honour, a pleasant frolicsome Girl of sixteen, would sometimes set me astride upon one of her Nipples; with many other Tricks, wherein the Reader will excuse me for not being over particular. (119)

In the juxtaposition of topics in this last passage, students might find another parallel. In *Gulliver* as in "The Lady's Dressing Room," the house of love is pitched in the place of excrement; sexuality tends to be viewed within the larger context of the body itself and of processes that Gulliver, like Strephon, finds increasingly abhorrent.

I have mentioned "The Lady's Dressing Room" because this short poem and a companion piece, "Cassinus and Peter," have proved helpful in introducing Swift and *Gulliver* to undergraduates and in getting them to ask questions about the text. The second poem (which, like the first, is readily accessible) recounts a conversation between two college sophomores, Cassinus and Peter, who consider themselves "special Wits, and Lovers both." Cassinus here experiences a deep depression after learning that his Caelia does a "Deed unknown to Female Race." She goes to the bathroom: "Nor wonder how I lost my Wits; Oh! *Caelia, Caelia Caelia* sh——" (*Poems* 2: 597). A teacher might begin here by asking what, specifically, Swift is satirizing. Is he attacking the female race and suggesting that different standards apply to women? (Cassinus, described as "well embrown'd with Dirt and Hair," is no model of cleanliness himself; his dorm room is equally a disaster.) Or is Swift satirizing male perceptions of females, not so much women as young men's ideas about women? If the latter, how are Cassinus's ideas about Caelia connected with his ideas about himself? Such questions can generate a lively class discussion, not only about topics undergraduates tend to find interesting (relationships), or about problems worthy of consideration (sexual politics), but about issues that can inform a student's reading of *Gulliver*. Not the least of these is the relation of sexuality and the body to larger Swiftian questions about perception and self-love.

In the poems, Cassinus and Strephon see their Caelias in one way at one time and in a very different way at another. Which is closest to the truth? Gulliver sees his wife one way before his last voyage, and another on his return. Which Mary Gulliver are we left with? Has she changed? Or has his perception of her? How we perceive the world, or fail to do so, is central to Swift. He often poses this problem by giving us a character who fails to see. Near the end of book 1, for instance, we find the giant Gulliver defending his innocence in an affair with a Lilliputian lady and ignoring the one fact that would have cleared them both immediately: size. More revealing, perhaps, is his response to the Laputan wives whose husbands are "so rapt in Speculation" that they need flappers to rouse them into any kind of response. The women "lament their Confinement to the Island" and will do anything to get off it—as in the case of the Laputan wife who ran away with "an old deformed Footman, who beat her every Day, and in whose Company she was taken *much against her Will*" (166; emphasis added). Why, a teacher might ask, would a woman prefer this treatment to a marriage to the richest Laputan? Or why, barring such escapes, would women on the island be so fond of strangers arriving "from . . . below"? One obvious answer students might give is that these women are physically and emotionally neglected. Being married to a Laputan is no fun. You might then point to what Gulliver wants the reader to get from this: "This may perhaps pass with the Reader rather for an *European* or *English* Story, than for one of a Country so remote. But he may please to consider, that the Caprices of Woman-kind are . . . much more uniform than can be easily imagined" (166). Is this a story of female caprice or male neglect? Probably to some extent both, though Gulliver's pleasure here in finding fault with women is consistent with his comments elsewhere. That Laputans engage in speculation at the expense of their wives is nonetheless obvious. That Gulliver fails to see this is equally obvious. Does Gulliver's blindness suggest something about Gulliver himself? In his adieu to the reader at the end of the *Travels*, Gulliver notes that he will now "return to enjoy my own Speculations in my little Garden at *Redriff*" (295). At this point, we know that Gulliver too is neglecting his wife. Do the relations between the Laputans and their wives mirror Gulliver's situation at home?

Whatever the case, being married to Gulliver is no fun. In book 1, he tells us how this marriage came about. While setting up a practice in London with the help of his master surgeon, Gulliver was advised to "alter my Condition" by marrying (20). In class, you might read his opening three paragraphs aloud and ask students who is Gulliver's master at this time. In the first, we learn it is "Mr. James Bates" and later "Mr. Bates," who becomes, in the second paragraph, "my good Master Mr. Bates" or "Mr. Bates, my Master," and, in the third, simply "my good Master *Bates* (19-20). This is not simply a classroom joke; it is Swift's (Fox). While he was writing *Gulliver*, there was near hysteria over the dangers of masturbation, sparked by a pamphlet titled *Onania: Or, The Heinous Sin of Self-Pollution, and All Its Frightful Consequences*. In *A Modest Defence of Publick Stews* (1724), for instance, Bernard Mandeville warns of the horrid effects of "Manufriction, *alias* Masturbation" (30-31); and the 1725 London edition of *Onania* would similarly speak of "licentious Masturbators" and that "cursed School-wickedness of Masturbation" (19-20). In 1726, is Gulliver's apprenticeship to "Master Bates" only a local joke? Or does it have wider significance? A work to which Swift contributed, the *Memoirs of Scriblerus*, may help. Here, in "The Case of a young Nobleman," masturbation is linked to self-love and to the tale of Narcissus (*Memoirs of Scriblerus*, ch. 11). The same is true in the *Travels*, where the opening play on masturbation takes on meaning within larger themes suggestive of Gulliver's response to his wife—and world.

When others try to love Gulliver, you might ask your class, what is his response? Does it have anything in common with his experience with his beloved Houyhnhnms? In both cases, rejection. This motif, the "frustrated love," is a central theme in *Gulliver* and in Ovid's account of Narcissus. The story in Ovid is the story not simply of Narcissus but also of Echo and the others who tried to love him. At a key moment in Ovid's tale, Echo sees Narcissus and, "inflamed with love," races up to "throw her arms around" him. He immediately "flees her approach," yelling "Hands off! embrace me not!" (*Metamorphoses* 1.3.390). In book 4 of the *Travels*, the same scene is comically reenacted in Gulliver's encounter with the Yahoo woman who, "inflamed by Desire," came "running with all Speed" up to him and "embraced me after a most fulsome Manner; I roared as loud as I could . . . whereupon she quitted her Grasp, with the utmost Reluctancy, and leaped upon the opposite Bank, where she stood gazing and howling" (266-67).

This version of the "frustrated love"—with Gulliver playing Narcissus to a Yahoo Echo—is picked up later in a series of embrace scenes that are not as comic. When Gulliver arrives home, for instance, he tells us that "my Wife took me in her Arms, and kissed me; at which, having not been used to the Touch of that odious Animal for so many Years, I fell in a Swoon for almost an Hour" (289). As in his encounter with the Yahoo Echo, Gulliver's rejection here is explicitly sexual. Under the direction of "Master Bates," Gulliver had been advised to alter his condition by marrying. Now, finally returning home, he laments that "by copulating with one of the *Yahoo*-Species, I had become a parent of more; it struck me with the utmost Shame,

Confusion, and Horror" (289). He does not let this happen in the future and continues to scorn his wife's embraces right up to the time he writes the book; in the five years he has been home, he has let no one in his family even "take me by the Hand" (290). Is Gulliver committing himself here at the end of the work to the Narcissus-like isolation evoked at the beginning, in his situation with his good Master Bates? The "frustrated love" works both ways. In Ovid, he who will not let others love him is doomed to a hopeless love himself, and to be tortured by the "unattainability of an idealized self-image" (Goldin 08). That image in the *Travels* is embodied in Gulliver's "Love and Veneration" (258) for the Houyhnhnms, who reject him just as he rejects the others.

If you ask students about Narcissus, they might recall the boy's preoccupation with himself in a pond. This "reflection" motif is central to the tale. In their adaptation of this myth in the *Memoirs*, Swift and his friends connect the "reflection" to the young man's masturbation and "Familiarities" with himself, to his absorption in a "looking-glass," and to a larger movement from self-love to self-hatred.

Are these same elements at work in *Gulliver*? We have seen Gulliver's fascination with and rejection of female bodies. What is his attitude toward his own? Is the opening play on "Master Bates" the only reference to Gulliver's own familiarities with himself? He does seem to enjoy telling us, for instance, about the young officers in Lilliput who march under his tattered trousers and look up not simply with "Laughter" but with "Admiration" (42). Elsewhere in the same book, he vividly describes his defecation and then feels the need to apologize for it, in order "to justify my Character in Point of Cleanliness to the World" (29). In a parallel passage in book 2, he tells us about it again and, in another apology, claims that this description will "help a Philosopher enlarge his Thoughts and Imagination" (94). How it will help is not clear. What is clear is that Gulliver dwells on such details throughout. And the ones he provides—his later defense of his own "Smell" (119), for example, or the "Shame" with which he views his sexual acts (289)—reveal a strange preoccupation with and a progressive hatred of his own body. This same pattern suggests itself in the references to mirrors, culminating in Gulliver's stark rejection of his human form in book 4: "When I happened to behold the Reflection of my own Form in a Lake or Fountain, I turned away my Face in Horror and detestation of my self; and could better endure the Sight of a common *Yahoo*, than of my own Person" (278). In a passage that evokes and also modifies the Narcissus myth, Gulliver—here as elsewhere—claims to hate his "Reflection" in mirrors. A similar modification of the myth appears in the *Fables* of La Fontaine, who gives us in "The Man and His Reflection" a Narcissus who avoids mirrors because they show him that he looks like everybody else and detract from his idealized conception of himself. Does Gulliver have similar motives? Mirrors do reflect the human form he has now rejected: a rejection arising, in part, from the Narcissus-like fascination with himself adumbrated throughout and in the opening play on masturbation.

Mirrors also detract from Gulliver's idea of what he wants to become. What he wants to become is a rational horse. Thus, in the same passage in book 4, you might note in class, Gulliver immediately turns away from his human "Reflection" to focus on another image—the Houyhnhnms—on which he looks "with Delight" (278). This image is evoked again at the end of the *Travels*, where we find Gulliver living "in great Amity" (290) with two "Stone-Horses": stallions to most people, but to Gulliver "idols" of his beloved Houyhnhnms. This image pleases Gulliver because it allows him to deny the human form he has rejected and to dream the dream of a purely rational life. Just as important, it enables him to "pretend to some Superiority" (293) over the rest of the human race. That this image is a delusion, however, is suggested by the disparity between what Gulliver wants to become and what he is. Attempting to live a life of pure reason, Gulliver loses it altogether—the references to madness abound. Attempting to escape his body, he ends up enmeshed in it, enjoying the fumes of his groom while unable to tolerate the smell of his own wife.

In the classroom, then, the motifs of sexuality and the body can be linked to Gulliver's self-love and to his attempt to get out of his body and become a purely rational being. In Swift, any such attempt inevitably leads to a fall. While satirizing the Laputans and their need for flappers, Swift brings in his favorite story, about a philosopher who looked up at the stars and tumbled into a privy (160). In Brobdingnag, Gulliver himself attempts to leap over a pile of dung "but unfortunately jumped short, and found my self just in the Middle up to my Knees" (124). Could this last detail, you might ask, be a type action for the entire work?

I thank the editors of *Eighteenth-Century Studies* for permission to reprint, in altered form, several sentences from my "Myth of Narcissus in Swift's *Travels*," *Eighteenth-Century Studies* 20 (1986): 17–33.

Gulliver the Dreamer

Dolores Palomo

Instead of locating *Gulliver's Travels* in a particular intellectual or political context, I try to humanize it as an everyman's story that tells us both what living in society is like and how society comes to be what it is: the imaginary lands Gulliver visits, after all, are reformulations and refractions of the England and Ireland that Swift knew, but in their follies and corruptions we also see the lineaments of our own world. Though we have all been trained to read the *Travels* as a satire and to treat Gulliver as a persona, the story nonetheless possesses certain novelistic qualities that can be used (I hesitate to say exploited) to lead students into the text in an especially penetrating way. *Gulliver's Travels* then becomes not simply a satire of assorted human follies but also the story of a human being's encounter with a smug and acquisitive society.

Usually I begin by pointing out Swift's several suggestions that Gulliver's remarkable voyages are rather like dreams. For example, at the beginning of book 4 Gulliver wakes up from yet another misadventure at sea:

> I feared my brain was disturbed by my sufferings and misfortunes: I roused myself, and looked about me in the room where I was left alone. . . . I rubbed my eyes often, but the same objects still occurred. I pinched my arms and sides, to awake myself, hoping I might be in a dream. I then absolutely concluded, that all these appearances could be nothing else but necromancy and magic. (Landa ed. 185)

Suppose, I suggest to students, that a psychiatrist listens to a new patient, a maritime surgeon named Lemuel Gulliver, tell about a dream in which he was shipwrecked and washed up all alone in a land populated by human beings six inches tall, a situation reversed in the next dream, when the patient turns into a six-inch dwarf stranded in a land of giants. Suppose further that the patient finally recounts four extensively detailed dreams in which he or she undergoes the experiences described in *Gulliver's Travels*. Students quickly begin to look at the voyages as if they were dreams that recapitulate the experiences and emotions of the dreamer's life. We observe that Gulliver's imaginary worlds contain frighteningly deformed images of human beings—absurdly little, fantastically huge, cockeyed, grossly defective, decrepit, ghostly, equine—and that the four "dreams" record progressive assaults on Gulliver's aspirations and self-esteem.

We can read these distortions as the telling products of bitter experience, an amalgam of Gulliver's feelings about himself and his fellow creatures. What has happened in Gulliver's life, I ask, to produce such feelings?

The innocuous factual details that Swift provides in the first paragraphs establish a revealing chronology, which students can be asked to work out for themselves. This exercise produces a schedule something like the following:

1661	Year of birth
1675	Attends Cambridge for 3 years, no degree
1678	Apprenticed to Bates for 4 years
1682	Attends medical school at Leyden for 2½ years, apparently no degree or license in surgery or medicine
1684-85	Signs on with the *Swallow*, 3½-year voyage
1688	Marries, settles in the Old Jewry, begins practicing surgery in London for 2 years, business begins to fail
1690	Goes to sea for 6 years with "some addition to my fortune," but the final voyage proves unfortunate
1696	Practices surgery in London for 3 years without success, moving from Old Jewry to Fetter Lane to Wapping
1699	First voyage of *Gulliver's Travels* (May 4)

For a man of thirty-eight who likes to impress on the reader his dignity and intellectual acumen, this is indeed a curriculum vitae distinguished by failures and incompletes. After such a history, Gulliver embarks upon his strange voyages—or begins to experience bizarre dreams.

As a therapist would look for clues to the dreams in the patient's account of his or her life, so at this point the class begins to examine Gulliver's prior life more closely. Swift has provided a number of small details that, like the minutiae in a scene by Hogarth, economically build a portrait of a particular type of character. In this explication, I bring to the class some specialized knowledge of the medical profession in Swift's time. While I do not inflict upon them the full details of some rather extensive and esoteric footnotes (which will appear in an article I hope to publish separately), students learn through this demonstration what one kind of scholarly research can contribute to the elucidation of a literary text.

The first significant event we note is Gulliver's degreeless departure from Cambridge to take up an apprenticeship in surgery. Unlike today, surgery then was not a prestigious profession but a trade (until 1744 surgeons still belonged to the Barber-Surgeons Company), and gentlemen, the mark of whom is the university education, did not engage in trade. Surgeons pulled teeth, let blood, lanced boils, and cut off limbs—all "mechanical" operations; at best they assisted doctors by doing their dirty work, and at worst they were thought to be quacks and exploiters. After Cambridge, Gulliver's apprenticeship to a surgeon thus represents a major comedown in the world, like dropping out of Harvard to take up welding.

Gulliver, moreover, possesses no credentials as a properly qualified surgeon: he did not complete his apprenticeship, does not (apparently) take the formidable qualifying exams needed to obtain a license to practice, and does not train with an established surgeon in a London hospital or as assistant to a qualified physician. Nothing prevented uncredentialed practitioners from setting up marginal practices among the poor or from gaining reputations as the purveyors of sensational if questionable cures; to Swift such quacks belonged in the same category as almanac makers and sidewalk preachers. Furthermore, naval surgeons were widely regarded as less than competent, and merchant service ranked lowest of all—I may here tell the class a little about Smollett and *Roderick Random*. Gulliver's reason for leaving Cambridge—economic necessity—does not bear up under historical scrutiny: a university student could exist modestly on £40 a year, whereas high apprenticeship entry fees were required in the better-paying occupations; in surgery this fee ranged from £100 to £250. These economic data were as well known to eighteenth-century readers as the costs of college education are today.

A few years later his family gives him a second chance, and off he goes to the University of Leyden, which he will also leave without a degree. Several details indicate Gulliver's affinities for science, dissent, and commerce. The Old Testament name "Lemuel" is typically Puritan; Gulliver attends Emmanuel College, known as the dissenter's academy since its founding, and later the University of Leyden, an institution identified with the moderns and with science; he lives first in Old Jewry in the heart of the City, then moves to Fetter Lane near a notorious independent church and very close to the Royal Society—he likes the neighborhood so well he buys a tavern there with the proceeds of his Lilliputian livestock. His departure from Cambridge represents the first downward step in a decline that ends in Wapping, a seamy dockside neighborhood below the Tower that catered to sailors, decidedly not the sort of place where an honest surgeon would set up practice, though it clearly offered fair pickings for quacks and prostitutes. Intellectually he has fallen from the traditional humanistic learning of the university into the materialistic aberrations of trade, dissent, and science.

The "dream" of Lilliput, therefore, can be understood as the fulfillment of wishes so repeatedly frustrated in real life. In Lilliput

Gulliver finds himself not merely a big man but an incredible prodigy in a world of diminutive midgets. He enjoys this dream of omnipotence, a fantasy bred by the reality of impotence, like a child whose miniature playthings reverse its real situation as helpless little creature in a world controlled by and scaled to adults. (I confess that to make this point about size I brought to class a set of figurines about four inches tall and placed them on the floor. "How would you feel if you were down there—or if you were living among people of that size?") Students quickly fall into the role of Gulliver's analyst and begin discovering details of his dreams that "make sense" when understood as the product of his anxieties and disappointments. My role consists of providing information, some starting assumptions, and a sense of direction so that they can embark on their own journeys through this wonderfully deft and subtle text.

Indeed, many fine points are generally ignored in the criticism. For example, when Gulliver retains his grand style as giant among pygmies after returning from Lilliput, we assume he is having trouble readjusting to people of normal size, but it has not been observed that when he returns from Brobdingnag, he does not continue to behave as a small person among giants. Rather, at the first sight of normal human beings he instantly abandons his role as little person and adopts the perspective of the giants. This minute detail can then lead to many other incidents that reveal Gulliver's predisposition to lord it over other people and to such related traits as his susceptibility to flattery and his desire to appear as important as possible.

The obvious antitheses of books 1 and 2 suggest the polarities of paranoia: fantasies of power and grandeur alternating with delusions of persecution and victimization, a conviction of the world's hostility together with a grandiose sense of self, and preoccupation with dominance and submission. Such opposites exaggerate normal human tendencies to inflate one's own worth and to suffer simultaneously from feelings of inadequacy. Dr. Johnson's casual remark about *Gulliver's Travels* that "when once you have thought of big men and little men, it is very easy to do all the rest" (Boswell 2: 319) is shrewder and less contemptuous than it appears—provided we recognize the complexities and possibilities suggested by bigness and littleness.

Gulliver attempts to conceal from himself his meanness and insignificance, yet that awareness haunts him: in Brobdingnag he would not look in a mirror because the comparison between himself and the giants "gave me so despicable a conceit of myself" (119). In England, he projects that diminished self-image onto others while blowing himself up. After Lilliput, one would suppose Gulliver content with all the money rolling in from the exhibition of minuscule sheep, but he becomes disgruntled when people of quality no longer come to see his curiosities. Despite his modest fortune, he still is not receiving the esteem he craves. Our therapist might recall here that Gulliver attributed his failure to establish himself as a surgeon to his moral superiority over his colleagues, just as on ship he flaunts his literary tastes when as ship's surgeon he actually ranked with the ship's carpenter and other rude mechanicals. In the same way, on his title page Gulliver describes himself as "First a SURGEON, and then a CAPTAIN of several SHIPS"—students can be asked to judge the accuracy of this claim.

In Houyhnhnmland Gulliver's anxiety reaches its most intense pitch as he sees in the Yahoos the realization of his degraded self-image and fears of rejection. Meanwhile he beholds the Houyhnhnms with dread and awe as the embodiment of all the wisdom, benevolence, and prestige that Gulliver desires for himself, yet the complete unlikeness of that equine face to his own impresses upon him the sheer impossibility of his aspirations. Terrified lest he be thrown into the Yahoo kennel, Gulliver must maintain Houyhnhnm approval, hoping that "they would condescend to distinguish me from the rest of my species" (224). Like the outsider craving acceptance by the insider, Gulliver persists in this longing, so damaging to self-esteem, to be something other than what he is. But because he really does see himself as a Yahoo, their fate is logically his fate: they are but reformulations of his repressed image of himself as a contemptible creature, and their condition as degenerate outcasts recalls his own decline from Cambridge to the City to Wapping.

As the Yahoo symbolizes Gulliver's degraded sense of self, so the Houyhnhnm originates in Gulliver's inflated self-image. His magnification of self is an attempt to deny or to exorcise the persistent apprehension of his own insignificance. By the end of book 4, however, Gulliver has experienced such a sequence of harrowing events—treachery, terror, exhaustion, indifference, captivity, abasement, shipwreck, mutiny, abandonment—that he can no longer sustain that swollen concept of self mirrored in the models he would emulate: the great persons with whom he delights to mingle, the heroes of the past, and the pleasing visions of himself as king, great lord, oracle of wisdom, and treasury of knowledge. These noble images of the human being as wise and benevolent creature have, monstrously yet comically, turned into the placid visage of the horse. Gulliver's ideal man has become an absurdity, a four-footed creature whose pretensions to refinement and learning are ludicrous. But Gulliver cannot admit this mockery of his ideal, for that ideal also reflects his deepest psychological dilemma, that double bind born of the desire for greatness in the world's eye and the haunting sense of personal insignificance. For what is Gulliver if not an ordinary nobody who dreams of becoming a somebody?

But it is precisely Gulliver's ordinariness—the typical middle-class Englishman with commonplace human frailties—that makes the ending of his story so perplexing: nice normal middle-class retirees don't end up chatting four hours a day with their horses. While Swift no doubt intends the philosopher of the stable as a joke, he is also deadly serious. Given human nature as Swift saw it but as Gulliver does not (especially in himself), Gulliver's absurd fate is wonderfully logical. Gulliver, the former projector, dissenter, and enthusiast of science, lacks right reason, or proper religious and intellectual understanding, in Swift's view the only corrective or balance to the perversities of human nature.

And thus unarmed Gulliver goes naked and alone into a world that offers successive rebuffs and threats. In book 1 the Lilliputians turn treacherous and betray him; in book 2 he endures fear and humiliation from beginning to end; as book 3 opens Gulliver, in distress beneath the island, begs admittance only to be later mortified by Laputan contempt. While some incidents in book 3 fit into the scheme in various contrasts between big and little, high and low, elevation and debasement, Swift deemphasizes Gulliver's inner experience in order to focus on the play of external events and to engage in some specific satires. Still, the magicians of Glubbdubdrib frighten Gulliver with their suddenly disappearing spectral servants; the historical visions, from which he anticipates such pleasure, turn into a series of disenchantments; and the reality of the Struldbruggs contrasts horrifyingly with his expansive vision of immortality. Finally, in book 4 he witnesses the human race as despicable and degraded; his estrangement from his cherished ideals and his once-great aspirations is comically represented by his total inability to become a horse.

At the end of his travels—or his dreams, who can say?—he remains so convinced of the evil designs of other people that he "cannot suffer a neighbor Yahoo in my company without the apprehensions I am yet under of his teeth or his claws" (238). For Lemuel Gulliver the world has not proved a kindly place. Nor did it for Jonathan Swift: students are usually interested to know that at midlife Swift also looked at his failed career and despaired. But the likeness ends there: Gulliver, blaming the human race, retreats misanthropically to his stables, but Swift wrote *Gulliver's Travels*, fought the copper pence, served the cause of Ireland, and enjoyed his friends. Unlike his creator, Gulliver lacks the kind of insight into himself as well as a perspective on human life that would allow him to transcend failure and become reconciled with his fellows.

council closely resemble those charges leveled against Swift's friends the Earl of Oxford and Viscount Bolingbroke by a parliamentary committee of secrecy (Quinlan 1321-25). Equally unexpected is Swift's parody of modern etymological criticism of the kind burlesqued in both *A Tale of a Tub* and the annotations of Pope's *Dunciad*. Like some nautical version of the critic Richard Bentley, Gulliver pedantically insists that *"Laputa* was *quasi Lap outed; Lap* signifying properly the dancing of the Sun Beams in the Sea, and *outed* a Wing, which however I shall not obtrude, but submit to the judicious Reader" (Davis ed. 162). This is sober and splendid nonsense and one can only conjecture as to where Gulliver came by his mastery of philology or as to what the "judicious Reader" could possibly have to say about Laputan etymology. Gulliver is also a master of fulsome panegyric, a literary bad habit that Swift had earlier burlesqued in *A Tale of a Tub*. Here in his own panegyric on the "most Mighty Emperor of *Lilliput*, Delight and Terror of the Universe, whose Dominions extend five Thousand Blustrugs (about twelve Miles in Circumference) to the Extremities of the Globe . . . " (43), Swift offers a comically exaggerated version of "the Style and Manner of" the Lilliputians (43), creatures who are clearly meant to represent contemporary Englishmen.

In his visit to Glubbdubdrib in the third voyage, Gulliver's conversations with the ghosts of Homer, Aristotle, and a gallery of other departed worthies echo those "Dialogues of the Dead" and "Visits to the Shades" that were a popular satirical genre in the eighteenth century. Such works invariably exploited visits to the underworld or imaginary conversations with the dead as a means of satirizing the living or of discovering through such supernatural means the "truth" obscured by historians and hagiographers. Thus Gulliver discovers "how the World had been misled by prostitute Writers," and he is particularly shocked at the "Roguery and Ignorance of those who pretend to write *Anecdotes,* or secret history" (199). Here Swift alludes to those "Secret Histories" like Delarivière Manley's popular *Secret History of Queen Zarah and the Zarazians* (1705), thinly veiled romans à clef that pretended to reveal the "real" story behind contemporary events, in this case the secret sins of Sarah Churchill, Duchess of Marlborough. While Gulliver decries this kind of writing, he is quite eager to write his own "Secret Histories" filled with the sordid adventures of the rich and famous (Keener; Boyce; Richetti 119-67).

Among those contemporary genres whose outlines are most apparent in *Gulliver's Travels*, the voyage to the Houyhnhnms in particular, is what has come to be known as the "rational Utopia," a work of

Parody in *Gulliver's Travels*

Roger D. Lund

Hugh Kenner's remark that *A Tale of a Tub* parodies "the book as a book" (37) might easily be extended to include *Gulliver's Travels* as well. Like the *Dunciad* and *The Beggar's Opera*, *Gulliver's Travels* traces its lineage to the Scriblerian project of ridiculing abuses in modern learning and derives its formal miscellaneity and much of its satiric energy from its exploitation of the conventions of other kinds of writing. As Edward Said points out, Swift was "really a writer of *paraliterature*" (52). Throughout the *Travels*, Gulliver draws attention to the self-consciously imitative character of his literary enterprise. His detailed introductory remarks on the location and state of the manuscript, his complaints about the bookseller's mutilation of the text, his coy promises of sequels to come, his intrusive allusions to the habits of other writers, indeed the very shape and appearance of the book, with its maps, illustrations, and copious prefatory matter, all draw attention to what books were like in the early eighteenth century. Part of the difficulty in teaching *Gulliver's Travels* arises from Swift's parodic exploitation of a number of literary genres that would have seemed familiar enough to his original readers but whose novelty and generic peculiarity have disappeared with the passage of time. To complicate matters, Swift does not always limit himself to the parody of literature. Without warning he gleefully echoes popular clichés and impersonates points of view that are apt to be unidentifiable to the modern student.

Scholars have demonstrated ways in which Swift's reading contributed both to the specific satire and the stylistic texture of *Gulliver's Travels*. Many of these sources are recondite, so fully integrated into the logic of Swift's satire that the average reader does not recognize those particular passages as imitations at all. (See, for example, Eddy; Voigt; Ehrenpreis, *Swift* 3: 458-59; Taylor, "Cyrano"; and Traugott, "Voyage.") For parody to succeed, however, the reader must recognize it for what it is—the conscious adoption and exaggeration of the conventions and stylistic excesses of identifiable literary works or genres. Although Swift draws widely on the events or characters of a vast number of individual literary "sources," his literary parody tends to focus not on particular works but on "kinds" of literature.

No form of writing is too obscure to escape Swift's notice. For example, the political allegory of the voyage to Lilliput is underscored by the stylistic imitation of official government documents. The articles of impeachment drawn up against Gulliver by the king's fiction in which a European traveler visits a land of perfect beings who become the standard by which he measures the shortcomings of his own society. In such narratives as Gabriel de Foigny's *La terre australe connue* (1676) or Denis Veiras's *L'histoire des Severambes* (1677-79), works Swift might easily have known, the heroes encounter tribes of virtuous Australians who live according to natural law, who think reasonably, and who consider their European visitor a lower form of life (Williams, *Age of Compromise* 179-82). Rational utopias tended to echo the optimistic rationalism of such philosophers as Leibniz, Hutcheson, and Shaftesbury and would be exploited by the French *Libertins* in support of their own assaults on traditional religious belief (Williams, *Age of Compromise* 179; also Wedel). In some measure Swift depends on his audience's familiarity with this subgenre as the base for his satiric attack. As Maynard Mack remarks, "Swift, whose aim in *Gulliver* is (among other things) to show the fatuity of this creed [i.e., optimistic rationalism], deliberately adopts the voyage genre of the enemy and turns it to his own ends" (112).

Gulliver's Travels also bears certain unmistakable resemblances to the novel, but it internalizes many conventions that we have come to identify with the genre. Although there is no evidence that Swift had ever read *Robinson Crusoe*, critics such as Ross (in *Swift and Defoe*) and Dennis have long pointed to the similarities between *Crusoe* and *Gulliver*. As Frederick R. Karl observes, both works involve "travel, shipwreck, abandonment, exotic adventure, strung-together narratives"; Karl raises the question why *Crusoe* is "labelled, without any difficulty, a novel," while *Gulliver* is "treated rather warily as a kind of mutation, neither novel nor not novel" (279). The answer may rest in Swift's subtle indications throughout *Gulliver's Travels* that while he may adopt many of the conventions of the novel, he does not take them all that seriously. For example, Gulliver treats the reader to detailed descriptions of his youth, education, marriage and family, the predictable raw material of the realistic novel. Then Swift implicitly undermines the inclusion of such domestic minutiae when upon Gulliver's return from Houyhnhnmland he faints at his wife's embrace, choosing instead to spend his time with "two young Stone-Horses" (290). Like such early novelists as Manley and Defoe, moreover, Gulliver claims not to make anything up and he responds angrily to those so "bold as to think my Book of Travels a meer Fiction out of mine own Brain" (8).

Perhaps the strongest link between the *Travels* and the developing tradition of the novel is Gulliver's insistence that he reports "only plain Facts" (292) and his strict attention to descriptive detail, a link that has led numbers of critics to remark on the accuracy of Gulliver's observations, particularly in his calculation of scale in the voyages to Lilliput and Brobdingnag. In the words of Walter Scott, "Even Robinson Crusoe (though detailing events so much more probable) hardly excels Gulliver in gravity and verisimilitude of narrative" (in Williams, *Critical Heritage* 293). By pointing out the inaccuracy and disproportion of Gulliver's observations, however, other critics have suggested that Swift's careful realism of presentation may itself be a trick on the reader, as much a part of the novelistic parody as Gulliver's capture by pirates and wounding by savages, or that mock-objective tone of voice that remains unchanged whether Gulliver is being trampled by Lilliputians, carried aloft in the arms of a capricious monkey, or showered by the excrement of the Yahoos (Brady, "Vexations and Diversions").

Indeed, the mock explicitness and relentless circumstantiality of Gulliver's account parodies these conventions of both the modern novel and those travel narratives that formed the most obvious model for the *Travels*. While working on *Gulliver*, Swift wrote that he had been reading "I know not how many diverting Books of History and Travells" (*Correspondence* 2: 430), lines echoed by Gulliver, who also claims to have "perused several Books of Travels with great Delight" but who soon develops "great Disgust against this Part of Reading, and some Indignation to see the Credulity of Mankind so impudently abused" (291). While Swift consumed great quantities of travel narrative, as John Richetti points out, "*Gulliver's Travels* was inspired in part by Swift's contempt for the vulgar credulity that nourished a popular form like the travel account" (60), a contempt for the "curious reader" that Swift translated into a kind of parody which took maximum advantage of his readers' credulity.

Swift alludes more directly and more frequently to contemporary travel narrative than to any other literary form. (See Sherbo for Swift's knowledge of travel literature.) In the prefatory "Letter from Capt. Gulliver to his Cousin Sympson" Gulliver credits Sympson with having "prevailed upon me to publish a very loose and uncorrect Account of my Travels; with direction to hire some young Gentleman of either University to put them in Order, and correct the Style, as my Cousin *Dampier* did by my Advice" (5). Here Gulliver claims kinship with the most popular works of contemporary travel literature: William Dampier's *A New Voyage round the World* (1691) and William Symson's *A New Voyage to the East Indies* (1715). The first was a purely factual account, while the second was a complete fabrication, a subgenre of travel narrative that Percy Adams has aptly described as "travel lies" (1). As an "imaginary voyage," *Gulliver's Travels* falls somewhere in between, sharing features of both the outlandish "travel lies" of the period and the more reputable accounts of such travelers as William Dampier.

Throughout *Gulliver's Travels* one notes the tension between delight and disgust that marks Swift's attitude toward his own reading and that emerges so clearly in his parody of travel narrative. For example, Gulliver consistently pours abuse on his rivals, and when it is suggested that he publish his own travel account, he contemptuously replies that "we were already overstocked with Books of Travels: That nothing could now pass which was not extraordinary; wherein I doubted, some Authors less consulted Truth than their own Vanity or Interest or the Diversion of ignorant Readers" (147). Of course, Gulliver goes on to add to this overstock, and like his fellow travelers, he is extremely sensitive (as well he should be) to all charges that his account is untrue. And while he may demand that all travel writers take an oath that all they "intended to write was absolutely true" (235), Gulliver has no trouble defending his own veracity:

> Thus, gentle Reader, I have given thee a faithful History of my Travels for Sixteen Years, and above Seven Months, wherein I have not been so studious of Ornament as of Truth. I could perhaps like others have astonished thee with strange improbable Tales; but I rather chose to relate plain Matter of Fact in the simplest Manner and Style; because my principal Design was to inform, and not to amuse thee. (291)

Gulliver's remarks on his own style clearly echo those of William Dampier, who claimed to be more concerned to provide "a Plain and Just Account of the true Nature and State of the Things described, than of a Polite and Rhetorical Narrative" (40). That Gulliver's pious claims to plain speaking and truthfulness come attached to descriptions of talking horses, flying islands, pygmies, giants, and men who never die ironically suggests Swift's regard for the veracity of those travelers he imitates. Of course, *Gulliver's Travels* advertises itself throughout as a genuine travel account, and Swift apparently delighted in the consternation that ensued. He reported (how seriously one can only guess) that "A Bishop here said, that Book was full of improbable lies, and for his part, he hardly believed a word of it" (*Correspondence* 3: 189).

Gulliver's Travels defines itself in opposition to the conventions of travel narrative even as it parodies them in the most specific ways. For example, Gulliver's claim that his "Story could contain little besides common Events, without those ornamental Descriptions of strange Plants, Trees, Birds, and other Animals; or the barbarous Customs and Idolatry of savage People, with which most Writers abound" (147) clearly reveals Swift's familiarity with the conventions of travel narrative and echoes the preface to *A Voyage to New-Holland* (1699). There Dampier remarks that his volume "may in some measure be acceptable to Candid and Impartial Readers, who are curious to know the Nature of the Inhabitants, Animals, Plants, Soil, &c. in those distant Countries" (39). Casting a glance toward the prolixity of travel narrative, Gulliver calls attention to his own mastery of "Sea-Language" (7). And his publisher, who allows that "The Author, after the Manner of Travellers, is a little too circumstantial" (9), draws our attention to the central stylistic fact of Gulliver's narrative: its superfluity of detail. Echoing Dampier's publisher almost word for word, Gulliver's publisher claims that the work would have been twice as long "if I had not made bold to strike innumerable Passages relating to the Winds and Tides . . . together with the minute Descriptions of the Management of the Ship in Storms, in the Style of Sailors: Likewise the Account of the Longitudes and Latitudes" (8-9; Bonner 163).

Such claims are meant to seem ridiculous, of course. Gulliver never raises sail without meticulously recording his latitude, longitude, wind direction, and time of day. He even goes so far as to correct the maps of his "worthy Friend, Mr. *Herman Moll*" (284), whose *New Correct Map of the Whole World* (1719) had provided the pattern for the maps in *Gulliver's Travels*. Gulliver, alas, is no cartographer, and if we take his reckonings seriously, Lilliput would be located somewhere in the Australian outback. While some scholars have argued that such an error was undoubtedly unintentional, it seems more likely that Swift would have taken delight in vexing the credulity of his readers just as he delighted in Arbuthnot's story of the "old Gentleman, who went immediately to his Map to search for Lilly putt" (*Correspondence* 3: 180; Case 52-55; Bracher). Gulliver's claims to brevity seem even more questionable in light of the voyage to Brobdingnag, which begins with an extended description of a storm at sea copied almost verbatim from *Sturmy's Mariner's Magazine* (Quintana, *Mind and Art* 296). Ellen Leyburn points out the "characteristic doubleness of intention" in such passages, how Swift "can mock the real mariner's concern with trifles and his reader's appetite for them, even while feeding and counting upon that appetite." The "parody is the more delightful because it is still half actually in the spirit of the original" (72).

Many of the early travelers had been sent out by the Royal Society on voyages of scientific exploration (Dampier was the first), and much of Gulliver's preoccupation with specific dates, times, and measurements imitates the scientific precision of their accounts. (See Frantz on eighteenth-century scientific travelers.) Gulliver's boast that his "sole intention" in publishing his *Travels* "was the PUBLIC GOOD" (235) echoes the triumphalism of the new science, most clearly articulated in Thomas Sprat's *History of the Royal Society* (1667) and most trenchantly parodied in Gulliver's voyage to Laputa. Swift's description of the flying island of Laputa was based on Sir William Gilbert's *De Magnete* (1600) and possibly a number of other pseudoscientific accounts of human flight (Nicolson and Mohler; Korshin). One certainty, however, is that Gulliver's "philosophical Account" (167) of the island's motion is a complex and clever parody of the kinds of reports published in the *Philosophical Transactions* of the Royal Society. Robert C. Merton has suggested that if one pays close attention to Gulliver's scientific explanation of the island's motion, one sees that it ought either to rotate or to crash, but it will not hover motionless above the ground as Gulliver asserts (276). While this may simply be a mistake, like the latitude and longitude of Lilliput, there is every reason to suppose that Swift's description of the flying island is yet another elaborate joke at his reader's expense, an exercise in literary parody that satirizes the attitudes and assumptions of scientific writers.

As a scientific traveler, one who has already donated curious specimens to the Royal Society, Gulliver might be expected to admire the scientific preoccupations of the Laputans. Hence we encounter an encomium on modern astronomy, a science for which Swift had no particular regard but for which Gulliver has boundless enthusiasm. "They have observed Ninety-three Comets, and settled their Periods with great Exactness," Gulliver exclaims. "If this be true, (and they affirm it with great Confidence) it is much to be wished that their Observations were made public; whereby the Theory of Comets, which at present is very lame and defective, might be brought to the same Perfection with other Parts of Astronomy" (171). In such a passage one hears echoes of the most uncritical champions of modern science, and Swift takes obvious delight in manipulating such "philosophic words" as *perihelion*, *effluvia*, and *nucleus* in his mock-scientific description. (For eighteenth-century scientific vocabulary, see Wimsatt.) But as usual there is a sharper satiric undercurrent below the more antic accents of Swiftian parody. These are, after all, the same astronomers who do their best work in a cave and who live in such perpetual fear of collision with a comet that they must secretly resort to astrologers to allay their fears for the future.

Swift's most trenchant satirical assault on the Royal Society comes in Gulliver's visit to the Academy of Lagado, where he encounters such perverse, bizarre, and seemingly senseless experiments as the attempt to extract sunbeams from cucumbers, to spin silk from spider webs, to "calcine Ice into Gunpowder" (180), and to plow "the Ground with

Hogs, to save the Charges of Plows, Cattle, and Labour" (180). Swift needed to invent very little; he had only to embellish or combine the actual reports published in the *Philosophical Transactions* to produce the antics of the scientific projectors of Lagado. As Marjorie Nicolson and Nora M. Mohler point out, Swift "simply set down before his readers experiments actually performed by members of the Royal Society, more preposterous to the layman than anything imagination could invent and more devastating in their satire because of their essential truth to source" (in Jeffares 254). Unlike his often playful adaptation of nautical language earlier in the *Travels*, however, Swift reveals less sympathy for modern science, its practitioners or its style. In his *History of the Royal Society*, Thomas Sprat had asserted that it was their intention to describe "so many *things*, almost in an equal number of *words*" (113); and in his description of the linguistic experiments of the Royal Academy of Lagado Swift implicitly ridicules such aspirations while calling into question Gulliver's own plain style. In those projectors who plan to substitute actual objects for words, who literally stagger under the weight of those things they wish to express, Swift found the perfect image to embody his contempt for the various stylistic pretensions of Sprat and the Royal Society.

The teacher and student should remember, however, that for Swift parody is seldom an end in itself. His imitation of various kinds of writing serves rather to underscore and to elaborate his satire on the writers themselves, or on the assumptions and motives that give rise to such modern forms as the travel narrative or the scientific report. At times, though, the parodic impulse seems irrepressible. And in order fully to appreciate the richness of Swift's satirical technique in *Gulliver's Travels*, one must never lose sight of Swift's "passion for hoaxing" and his "instinct for mimicry, parody, and self-dramatization" (Ehrenpreis, *Swift* 2: 331, 655).

Swift's Letters in Teaching Tone and Technique in *Gulliver's Travels*

Charles Pullen

A serious problem in teaching any Swift work lies in the fact that he requires his readers to know too much. In clearing up that problem, in establishing all the historical, political, religious, and social matrices that are essential to understanding all the allusions, there is little time left to deal with Swift as an artist, with that which distinguishes him in the long run from any lesser satirist of the period.

We are right in recognizing Swift as the great prose satirist of the period, even if we do not have the time to prove the claim. He is in the classroom not simply because he is a typical commentator on the intellectual concerns of his time but because he is the best of them. We read him because his subject matter is, more often than not, atypically expressed and is still today an artistic pleasure, as it was when originally written. What is difficult to convey is the nature of that "pleasure," not only because of our concern about factual detail but also because he is often very subtle. Little time is available to discuss "how" Swift is talking, constructing his satire, and that is where much of the real artistic power of Swift's work lies.

Swift has been judged, over and over again, to be less than a great thinker, so the secret of his artistic length and strength hardly lies there. Where does it lie? It lies in his ability to "fictionize" subjects, however obviously mundane they may be in the first instance, and however limited in topicality they may have become for the twentieth-century reader.

The ideal world would allow for some considerable reading in earlier works by Swift and some knowledge in depth of the *Journal to Stella* and the five volumes of letters edited by Harold Williams. Something less extravagant may be possible, in order to alert the perception of the novice reader to the density of the satiric works. A few letters might be read to a class to reveal the "real" Swift behind the *Travels* and also to show how tone and technique are constants in Swift's work and provide so much of the aesthetic power of his satires.

Landa's Riverside Gulliver's Travels *and Other Writings*, Greenberg's Norton *Travels*, and the Norton Critical Edition of the *Writings* (ed. Greenberg and Piper) contain modest selections of the letters, many of them with direct connections to the *Travels*, and in some of those letters there are modest examples of Swift's whimsy as a letter writer. The selections, however, show too little of the deeply ingrained playfulness and the creative energies in structure and tone that mark

Swift's correspondence. Students ought to know that Swift is always testing and teasing ideas and attitudes and that it is wise to watch for this mischief and tonal ripple in all his work—certainly in the *Travels*, where the multiplicity of satiric subjects may be so prevalent that the student fails to see how cleverly the ideas are written.

Indeed, if one had only a single letter to illustrate his deviousness, I would choose a fairly late letter, dated 28 January 1737–38 (*Correspondence* 5: 87–88). It reveals much about Swift's social side, which is often buried under the oversimplified idea that satirists are unsociable people and that Swift is particularly so. Perhaps the only clear thing about Gulliver's character is that he is a strongly social animal before he is destroyed by the rigors of the last voyage, and in that inclination he is very much like his maker.

The letter to Miss Richardson reveals how intensely social Swift was, and perhaps more to the point, how much he was liked and feted by his friends and, sometimes, slight acquaintances. But it also reveals something else: how aware Swift was of himself as a man honored for his literary gifts, and how he uses those talents to reward generosity. The Richardson letter is to a young woman whom he had never met but who had sent him a few shirts as a gift. Swift was often the recipient of gifts from strangers, and his response, in this particular case, is full of the sense of his pleasure and of his awareness of the opportunity to turn the banality of gratitude into art.

Miss Richardson's uncle had been kind to him on several previous occasions, and that fact, allied to Swift's delight in doing and saying things inappropriately, expressing ideas "upside down," and that inclination to carry ideas to their logical or illogical conclusion is clearly apparent in the letter. Any other person would have simply thanked the girl. Swift makes art out of it, beginning, right out of the box, in a manner reminiscent of John Donne, as if the heated conversation had been going on for some time:

> I must begin my correspondence by letting you know that your uncle is the most unreasonable person I was ever acquainted with; and next to him, you are the second, although I think impartially that you are worse than he. I never had the honour and happiness of seeing you, nor can ever expect it, unless you make the first advance by coming up to town, where I am confined by want of health; and my travelling days are over. I find you follow your uncle's steps, by maliciously bribing a useless man, who can never have it in his power to serve or divert you. (*Correspondence* 5: 87)

Swift is making a small drama out of a molehill of appreciation, taking the idea into areas that would not occur to the lay writer. It is just this ability to see the ramifications of an incident, not only for its thematic possibilities but for its tonal range, that is so often an important aesthetic aspect of the *Travels*, and that makes Samuel Johnson's comment about the big and little men so inane. What Swift does with simple ideas, situations, is the important thing, and the Richardson letter goes on to explore the long-term generosity of the uncle in a splendidly playful guise of paranoia that at the same time celebrates the kindness of this modest acquaintance: "However, your uncle came to me several times; and, I believe after several invitations, dined with me once or twice. This was all the provocation I ever gave him; but he had revenge in his breast, and you shall hear how he gratified it" (*Correspondence* 5: 87). The uncle had, in fact, honored Swift with gifts of usquebaugh, Spanish wine, and fresh salmon. "But what can I say of a man, who, for some years before I ever saw him was loading me every season with salmons, that surfeited me and all my visitors? Whereby it is plain that his malice reached to my friends as well as myself" (*Correspondence* 5: 87).

All this is simply a preliminary structure for Swift to use in order to thank the young woman for the shirts, but not before he has added to it further:

> At last, to complete his ill designs, he must needs force his niece into the plot; because it can be proved that you are his prime minister, and so ready to encourage him in his bad proceedings, that you have been his partaker and second in mischief, by sending me half a dozen of shirts, although I never once gave you the least cause of displeasure. (*Correspondence* 5: 87)

If everything is too small or too big or too irrational or too inhuman finally to make sense in the *Travels*, the same trick of seeing things through the wrong end of the telescope is implicit and occasionally explicit in the way Swift sees the Richardson gift, contextually and qualitatively upside down, which leads to an attack upon the character of the niece that is a splendid kind of baroque compliment.

> And, what is yet worse, the few ladies that come to the Deanry assure me, they never saw so fine linen, or better worked up, or more exactly fitted. It is a happiness they were not stockings, for then you would have known the length of my foot. Upon the whole, Madam, I must deal so plainly as to repeat, that you are more cruel even than your uncle; . . . I have seen some persons who live in your neighbourhood, from whom I have inquired into

your character; but I found you had bribed them all, by never
sending them any such dangerous presents: For they swore to
me, that you were a lady adorned with all perfections, such as
virtue, prudence, wit, humour, excellent conversation, and even
good housewifery; which last is seldom the talent of ladies in this
kingdom. (*Correspondence* 5: 87–88)

The extravagant twist of logic in the idea of bribing by not doing so
is typical of Swift in his letters and should prepare a reader for the
peculiar political reasoning of the school of Political Projectors.

The letter does not end there; it flows teasingly forward on the
remark about the limited talent of Irish ladies. He uses that idea to
take on a favorite guise of schoolmasterly chastisement with just a hint
of that sexuality that peeps through occasionally in the *Travels*,
particularly where nothing of serious satiric weight is being explored.
When the question of abolishing speech appears in book 3, chapter 5, a
similar Swiftian tickling of the domestic world slips in:

And this Invention would certainly have taken Place, to the very
great Ease as well as Health of the Subject, if the Women in
Conjunction with the Vulgar and Illiterate had not threatened to
raise a Rebellion, unless they might be allowed the Liberty to
speak with their Tongues, after the Manner of their Forefathers:
Such constant irreconcileable Enemies to Science are the Common People. (Davis ed. 11: 185)

This kind of pawkiness is common in the letters and shows up
occasionally in the *Travels*. When it does appear in the *Travels*, it is
often woven into more serious subject, and may be missed. When it is
missed, much of the galvanic energy that pushes the work past
diatribe into aesthetic pleasures can also be missed.

The Richardson letter, for instance, takes that constant of his
correspondence, the male-female battle, from mild insult through
slender sexual suggestiveness into a compliment that brings the letter
to a sonorous close:

So that when I see any of your sex, if they be worth mending, I
beat them all, call them names, until they leave off their follies,
and ask pardon. And, therefore, because princes are said to have
long hands, I wish I were a prince with hands long enough to beat
you at this distance, for all your faults, particularly your ill
treatment of me. However, I will conclude with charity. May you
never give me cause to change, in any single article, the opinion
and idea I have of your person and qualities. May you very long

continue the delight of your uncle and your neighbours round, who deserve your good-will, and of all who have merit enough to distinguish you. I am, with great respect and the highest esteem, Madam, Your most obedient and Most obliged humble servant. (*Correspondence* 5: 88)

Swift's letters, like his satires, function in many ways. This letter, beginning feet first in mock chagrin, exploring testily the generosity of the uncle, the deepening conspiracy of kindness, the quality of the shirts, and the character of the young woman, prowls in witty coyness, descending ever so slightly, to that game of women as naughty inferiors whom Swift must handle, reluctantly, for their own good, ascending in the end to the mock solemnity of the last few lines.

His letters regularly display this kind of tonal, structural, and stylistic "game." The significant thing is that the letters still stand up today for much the same reasons that the satires maintain artistic longevity. What the Richardson letter alerts us to is the sinuousness of his work, the stylistic and tonal energies he was prepared to expend in the simplest of social tasks. On occasion, there can be a homely silliness about the letters that readers of the more formidable works might think to be beneath Swift:

> I can send you no News; only the Employment of my Parishioners may for memory-sake be reduced under these Heads, Mr. Percivall is ditching, Mrs. Percivall in her Kitchin, Mr. Wesley switching, Mrs. Wesley stiching, Sr. Arthur Langford, riching, which is a new word for heaping up Riches; I know no other Rhime but Bitching, and that I hope we are all past. Well Sir, long may you live the Hospital Owner of good Bits good Books and good Buildings. (*Correspondence* 1: 163)

On many other occasions, that quick, economical insight into the political world that is particularly strong in books 1 and 2 of the *Travels* will appear:

> Besides, to say the truth, although I have known many great Ministers ready enough to hear Opinions, yet I have hardly seen one that would ever descend to take Advice; and this pedantry ariseth from a maxim themselves do not believe at the same time they practice by it, that there is something profound in Politicks, which men of plain honest sense cannot arrive to. (*Correspondence* 2: 369)

This comment is, ironically, similar to the kind of thing that Gulliver says in book 2 when the king listens but rebuffs him, and it is another example of the way Swift turns ideas upside down—as in book 2, when Gulliver is obviously doing the wrong thing, however reasonable he may sound.

Of course, the letters are not all disdain and irony. Often they are high-jinks and sheer silliness. Indeed, if one needs an explanation for the ideal of the horse in book 4, it might well lie, in part, in Swift's constant concern and affection for horses, which pervade the letters. They are a bit of comedy in themselves for him, even when he insists that he only keeps them for exercise. Buying them, naming them (one is named after St. John Bolingbroke), training them, feeding them, having them ruined by his grooms, haggling for them are constants in the letters. "I hunted four years for horses, gave twenty six pounds for one of three years and a half old, have been eighteen months training him, and when he grew fit to ride, behold my groom gives him a strain in the shoulder, he is roweled, and gone to grass. Shew me a misfortune greater in its kind" (*Correspondence* 2: 348).

He loved to travel in style with two mounted servants, and one of his finest examples of narrative economy, his ability to make a scene quiver with life in small, which often appears in the *Travels* (the first Gulliver-Yahoo meeting, for instance), can be seen in this confrontation:

> It was near 3 before I crosst the Ferry. There Tom and the Groom waited, and my Horses were standing at a Shop where Brandy is sold: at the door of it, I used to take Horse. I observed the two Loobyes put on my Cloak the wrong side outwards, and I found Will was drunk: I found Tom did not come up, I stayd, he galloped up; I chid him, he answered foolishly, he was drunk as a Dog, tottered on his Horse, could not keep the way, sometimes in the Sea, then back to me, swore he was not drunk, I bid him keep on, at last with galloping and turning backwards & forwards Bolingbroke grew mad, & threw him down, I came up, & called a Boy and Man to get the Horse from him, he resisted us all 3, was stark mad with drink, at last we got the Bridle from him, the Boy mounted, and away we rode, Tom following after us; what became of him I know not, I fancyed he would reel hither. (*Correspondence* 2: 153)

Even when he is ill, tired, and lonely, he can make a letter pop with energy, with the same kind of nervous intensity that we find in Gulliver's introductory letter to the *Travels*. Here, however, it is, in part, a compliment to the charms of one Mrs. Pendarves:

> I have observed among my own sex, and particularly in myself, that those of us who grow most insignificant expect most civility,

and give less than they did when they possibly were good for something. I am grown sickly, weak, lean, forgetful, peevish, spiritless, and for those very reasons expect that you, who have nothing to do but to be happy, should be entertaining me with your letters and civilities, although I never return either. . . . *It is your fault*; why did you not come sooner into the world or let me come later? *It is your fault* for leaving it. I confess your case if hard, for if *you return* you are a great fool to come among *beggars and slaves*, and if you do not, you are a *great knave* in forsaking those you have seduced to admire you. (*Correspondence* 4: 297)

What you ought to do is spend a pleasant few hours skimming the Williams edition, finding your own anticipations, echoes, and parallels. Swift can be as tough as old boots on his enemies in letters where that quickness of apprehension and skeptical breadth reminds one of the many ways the satire will suddenly focus icily in the *Travels*. On other occasions, he can be completely unbuttoned, can make a fool of himself in punnings and word fracturings that bring to mind Gulliver's amused awareness that the crotch of his breeches has badly thinned and that even hardened soldiers, passing between his legs in military review in Lilliput, ought not to be allowed to look up: "And, to confess the Truth, my Breeches were at that Time in so ill a Condition, that they afforded some Opportunities for Laughter and Admiration" (42). Reading a few of the letters may prepare students for the hilarious weight in the words "some" and "Admiration." Even a modest selection of the letters will leave them with an understanding of just how powerful Swift is as a manipulator not only of ideas but of language.

Gulliverian a...
Ways of Reading *Gull i...*

Jeanne K. Wel c...

The challenge of *Gulliver's Travels*—to   al... l...
teachers—is how and how not to read t...
tend in large measure to see the chall en...
confronted by something of an Ancient. Ye...
at one time or another, had a student as...
day get out of *Gulliver's Travels*?" Eve n...
querulousness, this question usually mak es...
have known so little about the receptio n...
the kinds of places where we have look ed... b...
records of literary comment—were ra... it... j...

But in fact pertinent eighteenth-cent ur...
another sort, that arose out of a reacti on...
Gulliver's Travels, the urge to prod uc...
Gulliverian pamphlet puts it, *A Little*   ...
categorized as imitations of *Gulliver's T ra*...
ana, they document copiously the v... a...
contemporaries read the book, the   a...
referred to it, the diverse media in...
vivacious responses.

Each piece of Gulliveriana has it s...
propagandistic aim, but all of them als o...
ately or un-self-consciously, as literary cr...
they evaluate *Gulliver's Travels*. Or th ey...
convey views that are personal, sponta ne...
In style, they play back something of   t...
lence, and passion of Swift's creatio n... .

Modern examples show the potentia l.
Deon (French), T. H. White and Mat t...
Karinthy (Hungarian), and Jakov Lin d...
length Gulliverian utopias, satires, je ux...
new stature in "The Voyages of a Mile — I...
by Judith Johnson Sherwin. Nigeria n...
poem about "Gulliver" serving a "Li l ly...
appears in satiric cartoons, as an astro n...
in Charles Addams's *New Yorker* cov er...
1985 as the United States at the merc y...
Loen's drawing *Gulliver* (18) the li n...
serves to define it. Jose Reissig app li...

and give less than they did when they possibly were good for something. I am grown sickly, weak, lean, forgetful, peevish, spiritless, and for those very reasons expect that you, who have nothing to do but to be happy, should be entertaining me with your letters and civilities, although I never return either. . . . *It is your fault*; why did you not come sooner into the world or let me come later? *It is your fault* for leaving it. I confess your case if hard, for if *you return* you are a great fool to come among beggars and slaves, and if you do not, you are a great knave in forsaking those you have seduced to admire you. (*Correspondence* 4: 297)

What you ought to do is spend a pleasant few hours skimming the Williams edition, finding your own anticipations, echoes, and parallels. Swift can be as tough as old boots on his enemies in letters where that quickness of apprehension and skeptical breadth reminds one of the many ways the satire will suddenly focus icily in the *Travels*. On other occasions, he can be completely unbuttoned, can make a fool of himself in punnings and word fracturings that bring to mind Gulliver's amused awareness that the crotch of his breeches has badly thinned and that even hardened soldiers, passing between his legs in military review in Lilliput, ought not to be allowed to look up: "And, to confess the Truth, my Breeches were at that Time in so ill a Condition, that they afforded some Opportunities for Laughter and Admiration" (42). Reading a few of the letters may prepare students for the hilarious weight in the words "some" and "Admiration." Even a modest selection of the letters will leave them with an understanding of just how powerful Swift is as a manipulator not only of ideas but of language.

Gulliveriana
Ways of Reading *Gulliver*

Jeanne K. Welcher

The challenge of *Gulliver's Travels*—to all
teachers—is how and how not to read the
tend in large measure to see the challen
confronted by something of an Ancient. Yet
at one time or another, had a student ask,
day get out of *Gulliver's Travels*?" Even
querulousness, this question usually makes
have known so little about the reception
the kinds of places where we have looked
records of literary comment—were rariti

But in fact pertinent eighteenth-century
another sort, that arose out of a reaction
Gulliver's Travels, the urge to produce
Gulliverian pamphlet puts it, *A Little M*
categorized as imitations of *Gulliver's Tra*
ana, they document copiously the vari
contemporaries read the book, the ab
referred to it, the diverse media in w
vivacious responses.

Each piece of Gulliveriana has its o
propagandistic aim, but all of them also f
ately or un-self-consciously, as literary crit
they evaluate *Gulliver's Travels*. Or they i
convey views that are personal, spontaneo
In style, they play back something of the
lence, and passion of Swift's creation.

Modern examples show the potential. A l
Deon (French), T. H. White and Matthe
Karinthy (Hungarian), and Jakov Lind (A
length Gulliverian utopias, satires, jeux d
new stature in "The Voyages of a Mile-High
by Judith Johnson Sherwin. Nigerian poe
poem about "Gulliver" serving a "Lillyw
appears in satiric cartoons, as an astronaut
in Charles Addams's *New Yorker* cover (
1985 as the United States at the mercy of
Loen's drawing *Gulliver* (18) the line t
serves to define it. Jose Reissig applied

and give less than they did when they possibly were good for something. I am grown sickly, weak, lean, forgetful, peevish, spiritless, and for those very reasons expect that you, who have nothing to do but to be happy, should be entertaining me with your letters and civilities, although I never return either. . . . *It is your fault*; why did you not come sooner into the world or let me come later? *It is your fault* for leaving it. I confess your case if hard, for if *you return* you are a great fool to come among *beggars and slaves*, and if you do not, you are a *great knave* in forsaking those you have seduced to admire you. (*Correspondence* 4: 297)

What you ought to do is spend a pleasant few hours skimming the Williams edition, finding your own anticipations, echoes, and parallels. Swift can be as tough as old boots on his enemies in letters where that quickness of apprehension and skeptical breadth reminds one of the many ways the satire will suddenly focus icily in the *Travels*. On other occasions, he can be completely unbuttoned, can make a fool of himself in punnings and word fracturings that bring to mind Gulliver's amused awareness that the crotch of his breeches has badly thinned and that even hardened soldiers, passing between his legs in military review in Lilliput, ought not to be allowed to look up: "And, to confess the Truth, my Breeches were at that Time in so ill a Condition, that they afforded some Opportunities for Laughter and Admiration" (42). Reading a few of the letters may prepare students for the hilarious weight in the words "some" and "Admiration." Even a modest selection of the letters will leave them with an understanding of just how powerful Swift is as a manipulator not only of ideas but of language.

Gulliveriana:
Ways of Reading *Gulliver's Travels*
Jeanne K. Welcher

The challenge of *Gulliver's Travels*—to all readers but especially to
teachers—is how and how not to read the book. Understandably we
tend in large measure to see the challenge as one of we Moderns
confronted by something of an Ancient. Yet I suspect that we have all,
at one time or another, had a student ask, "What did people in *Swift's*
day get out of *Gulliver's Travels*?" Even when voiced with minimal
querulousness, this question usually makes teachers back off. Why we
have known so little about the reception of *Gulliver's Travels* is that
the kinds of places where we have looked for answers—book reviews,
records of literary comment—were rarities during Swift's lifetime.

But in fact pertinent eighteenth-century records abound, records of
another sort, that arose out of a reaction frequent among readers of
Gulliver's Travels, the urge to produce, as the title of a 1727
Gulliverian pamphlet puts it, *A Little More of That Same*. Loosely
categorized as imitations of *Gulliver's Travels* and known as Gulliveriana, they document copiously the varied ways in which Swift's
contemporaries read the book, the abundance with which they
referred to it, the diverse media in which they expressed their
vivacious responses.

Each piece of Gulliveriana has its own design and artistic or
propagandistic aim, but all of them also function, however indeliber-
ately or un-self-consciously, as literary criticism. Patently or deviously,
they evaluate *Gulliver's Travels*. Or they inferrably interpret it. They
convey views that are personal, spontaneous, wide-ranging in allusion.
In style, they play back something of the originality, magic, ambiva-
lence, and passion of Swift's creation.

Modern examples show the potential. Akutagawa (Japanese), Michel
Deon (French), T. H. White and Matthew Hodgart (British), Frigyes
Karinthy (Hungarian), and Jakov Lind (Austrian) have written book-
length Gulliverian utopias, satires, jeux d'esprit. Glumdalclitch gains
new stature in "The Voyages of a Mile-High *Fille de Joie*," a short story
by Judith Johnson Sherwin. Nigerian poet Wole Soyinka has done a
poem about "Gulliver" serving a "Lillywhite King." Captive Gulliver
appears in satiric cartoons, as an astronaut pinned down by moon men
in Charles Addams's *New Yorker* cover (14 June 1958), repeatedly in
1985 as the United States at the mercy of tiny terrorists. In Alfred Van
Loen's drawing *Gulliver* (18) the line that entangles the body also
serves to define it. Jose Reissig applied the name to morphological

mutants for "giving rise to giant ('gulliver') colonies" (Terenzi and Reissig). In 1978 discount stores in France sold kits—pictures of Lilliput together with colored transfers—for a child to make illustrations, for example, imprinting pictures of Lilliputian provisioners onto a sketch of Gulliver, a prostrate seventeen-year-old, impeccably dressed, openmouthed, serenely awaiting lunch. Twentieth-century Gulliveriana have their value in the classroom.

The Gulliveriana produced before the early nineteenth century, however, have a special character, being the work of Swift himself, his contemporaries, his immediate successors. Extant today are more than six hundred responses produced by hundreds of writers, theatrical producers, and artists. There are full-length books, pamphlets, periodical essays, verses, broadsides, personal letters, plays, a song in a play, dances and other theatrical performances, sketches and drawings, paintings, frontispieces, illustrations, woodcuts and engravings, individual prints and multiple sets, and at least one item of kitsch—hand-painted "Lilliputian fans," known today only from 1727 advertisements. These Gulliveriana were done by amateurs and professionals, writing in eleven languages, in fourteen countries, over the course of nearly a century. After 1800 their nature altered and their frequency declined.

The phenomenon of Gulliveriana was no happenstance. Swift's earlier writings elicited stormy reactions, not altogether welcome. With *Gulliver's Travels* he decided to engineer the response, deliberately to provoke an outcry—pro and con. By mockery and hyperbole, he created positive and negative models of how to read *Gulliver's Travels*. "I have left the Country of Horses, and am in the flying Island," Swift wrote Charles Ford (19 Jan. 1724; *Correspondence* 3: 5). His friends caught his spirit of self-imitation, echoed it for his delight, passed it on. The genuine alter egos of Swift entered into mock complicity with Gulliver. The fake ones functioned as Gulliver clones, producing verbal and visual expositions of their own Gulliverian credulity, vanity, hasty judgment. They read by projecting into the text their own images and beliefs. Their works show that Swift's creation was no exaggeration.

Until recently Gulliveriana made rare classroom appearances because their scope was virtually unknown, copies were scarce, scholarship almost nonexistent (see Eddy 193–203; Teerink, nos. 1215–75; Goulding 56–103; Brengle, ch. 6; Lenfest, "Checklist"; and scattered references in Gove and in Stephens and George). Gulliveriana are increasingly available in separate editions, in the authors' or artists' collected works, and reprinted in the series *Gulliveriana I–VI* (see *Gulliveriana* series: *Gulliveriana I–VI*, facsimile reprints of texts;

Gulliveriana VII [forthcoming], pictures; *Gulliveriana VIII*, annotated list of all eighteenth-century imitations, bibliography, index). Primary and secondary materials can be turned to account in ways of which the following are samples that have worked well.

1. Attitudes toward *Gulliver's Travels*. Many reactions of eighteenth-century readers are those of readers in general. Unlike what is expressed in the classroom, Gulliveriana have a distance and impersonality that facilitate objective discussion and appraisal. Also, whereas statements about *Gulliver* either by students or academicians are often minimally or overly articulate, repetitious, deadening, the approach of these works is imaginative, lively, provocative.

A week after *Gulliver's Travels* was published Arbuthnot congratulated Swift, saying "Gulliver is a happy man that at his age can write such a merry work," telling of Princess Caroline's laughter at the oddly heeled Prince, and contributing surely invented, now classic anecdotes about credulous readers (5 Nov. 1726; *Correspondence* 3: 179–80). For almost a century *Gulliver* met the same kind of merriment and tribute. Pope, in his *Verses on the Occasion of Mr. Gulliver's Travels* (1727), attributed to Glumdalclitch a bathetic lament for Gulliver; Fielding transformed her into Glumdalca, the captive Queen of the Giants who pines for Tom Thumb (1730). Walpole high-spiritedly lived in Lilliput, identified with Gulliver, became a Struldbrugg, personally saw Houyhnhnms, or so his letters say (Welcher, "Walpole"). Humor characterizes LeFebvre's illustrations of 1797 (Lenfest, "LeFebvre's Illustrations"). Lady Bolingbroke, Cruikshank, Diderot, Franklin, Gay, Eliza Haywood, Holberg, Marivaux, Voltaire, the publisher of Raspe's *Baron Munchausen*, and a host of lesser and unknown Gulliverianists laughed appreciatively as well as sardonically and helped others to laugh along with them.

Minor reactions were more diversified. Swift's fellow alumnus Bishop Jonathan Smedley denounced the book with gusto: "*Gulliver's Travels*! An abominable Piece! by being quite out of Life! The Fable is entirely ridiculous; the *Moral* but ludicrous; the *Satire* trite" (xix). He turned what made it popular, its comedy, into a fault: "his best Quality is no better than that of the *Tarantula*: It causes Laughter, but it also causes Death to the Understanding" (268; see also 1–10, 279–82, 329–32). Bolingbroke, supposedly one of Swift's closest friends, was alone in expressing an even darker view: "Every great genius borders upon folly," he wrote to Charles Ford; but for Stella,

> our poor friend would have wander'd from one ideal world to another, and have forgot even the species he is of. He had been att this very instant perhaps . . . a bell under his chin, a plume on

his head, and a fox-tail att each ear, in that country which he discover'd not long ago, where Horses & mules are the reasonable Creatures, and men the Beasts of burden. (25 Dec. 1723, missent to Swift; Swift, *Letters . . . to Charles Ford* 238)

And indeed the ghost of Gulliver can readily be found wandering "from one ideal world to another" in many a utopia and dystopia. Some wittily inventive ones are *Memoirs of the Court of Lilliput, Voyage to Cacklogallinia, Ile de la Folie* (all 1727), *A Trip to the Moon by McDermot* (1728), Holberg's *Journey to the World Underground* (1741), Voltaire's *Micromegas* (1752).

2. Interpretations of *Gulliver's Travels*. By reading selected Gulliveriana or simply by reading about them, teacher and student can find a range of answers on how to interpret *Gulliver*, a range of fresh questions. How old is Gulliver before and after his travels and what difference does it make? The visual artists necessarily committed themselves on this question and some writers followed suit with a Gulliver who grew younger with the years. Other issues: How significant were Swift's sources? Are Yahoos human beings? What role do women play in *Gulliver's Travels*? Is the book intended for children?

Five pamphlets that are clearly the work of Swift and his friends (*It Cannot Rain but It Pours* and its sequels, 30 Apr. 1726–Aug. 1727) highlight two Gulliverian topics, rarities and faction. Their approach is by way of current examples: competitive Italian opera singers, Peter the Wild Boy who converses with horses, a London visit by "the Copper-Farthing Dean," Mist-Cibber feuds, and a contemporary sideshow featuring a rope-sliding ass (identified as a Houyhnhnm). The implicit thesis, frequent also in the Scriblerian letters, is that polarized attitudes and the rage for novelty are not passing objects of satire for Swift but an omnipresent preoccupation, a central unifying theme, from Gulliver's motivating restlessness to his ultimate alienation.

Gulliverianists by their imitation spotlight the satire of *Gulliver's Travels*. Swift's slaps at pedantry gain prominence in the persons of Bullum, an archetypally obstructive Library-Keeper (*An Account of the State of Learning*, 1727), and Dr. Bantley, a specialist in classical antiquities who defends the reality of Houyhnhnms to the last footnote (*Critical Remarks on Capt. Gulliver's Travels*, 1735). Though critics rarely cite freedom of expression as a Gulliverian issue, when a pamphlet war developed in Dublin because of censorship at Trinity College (1730–31), the pseudonym "Martin Gulliver" was devised for the spokesman of the opposition. Similarly, after the government banned publication of parliamentary debates, *Gentlemen's Magazine* (1738 46) invented Gulliver's grandson to provide almost monthly reports on "Lilliputian" debates—in the main, transcriptions of genuine speeches in Parliment with names and topics anagrammatized, largely the work of Samuel Johnson.

Innovations in Gulliveriana reveal subtexts in *Gulliver's Travels*—real and imaginary. Cartoonists associated Gulliver and John Bull (e.g., Stephens and George 7: 466, 614). *The Grub-Street Journal* and Fielding saw Gulliver as bookseller to Grub Street, a full-fledged hack—depreciated, yet envied by real Grubeans. Gullivers play the stock market in the spurious third volume of *Travels into Several Remote Nations* and in *Modern Gulliver's Travels* (1727; Welcher, "Gulliver in the Market-Place").

More varied was the reading of Swift on matters scientific. Lynceus Lilliput, a projector, writes playfully to the *Grub-Street Journal* about his minifying spectacles (1735). The Neapolitan *Un lezione su d'un vitello a due teste delle Accademico delle Scienze colle note di Lemuel Gulliver* (1745) ably parodies a current, earnest scientific essay on freaks of nature. *The Anatomist Dissected*, while comical in concept, argues unironically that indeed Mary Tofts did not give birth to rabbits (1726). Publishers of didactic works, even some for adults, took for granted that Gulliver's name would increase the marketability of tracts on natural history and Newtonian physics.

3. Close reading of *Gulliver's Travels*. Comparing a specific piece of Gulliveriana with the relevant passage or technique in *Gulliver's Travels* focuses attention on the fidelity to the original, the changes made, and the significance for readers of Swift's work.

Garrick's *Lilliput* (1756), a farce afterpiece built on Gulliver's attempt "to vindicate the Reputation of an excellent Lady" (Davis ed. 65), quite overthrows the defense. David Daggett's Fourth of July speech "Sun-Beams May be Extracted from Cucumbers, but the Process is Tedious" (1799) parallels American political projectors with Lagadan scientists. Curll's *A Key* is one of several paragraph-by-paragraph analyses of *Gulliver's Travels*, while *A Blunder of All Blunders: Or, Gulliver Devour'd by Butterflies* mocks "decypherers and commentators" who lay "Poor Lemuel . . . upon the Table" for examination, dissection, a coffee-house snack (both 1726). Frontispieces and illustrations (see Swift, *Annotated* Gulliver's Travels; Holly 146–50) contrast interestingly with the texts pictured.

Perhaps the richest single piece of Gulliveriana in terms of the number, variety, and compactness of allusions is Hogarth's *The Punishment of Gulliver* (1726; Hogarth, pl. 112; see Welcher, "Swift-Hogarth"). Hogarth's Lilliputians concoct as punishment a genuine if ill-advised reversal for Gulliver's "Urinal Profanation of the Pallace"—an enema. Among other Gulliverian details are the scale, which merges Lilliputian and Brobdingnagian proportions. The instrument used, which may be a giant clyster or a fire extinguisher, recalls Lagadan inventions. The image of bare-buttocked Gulliver on his knees is a montage of a horse's backside and Gulliver's groveling farewell to his Houyhnhnm master.

Certain passages in *Gulliver's Travels* evoked repeated eighteenth-century responses. The capture of sleeping Gulliver—seen only indirectly in *Gulliver's Travels*, because of the first-person narration (21, 27)—can be compared in illustrations by Bleyswick and LeFebvre (Lenfest, "LeFebvre's Illustrations," nos. 2, 11), two drawings by Richard Wilson (Welcher and Joseph), and Goya's red-chalk *Head of a Sleeping Giant* (Malraux 177). Likewise the repeated references to war in *Gulliver's Travels* were diversely received. Marie Antoinette Fagnan and Walpole wrote frothy fairy tales about wars between neighboring nations: *Kanor* (1750) and "Sequel to *Gulliver's Travels*" (1771). Sawrey Gilpin made a romantic painting of *Gulliver Reprimanded and Silenced by His Master When Describing the Horrors of War* (1772; see Duthie 130; Riely). Cartoons from 1786 through 1807 combined Gulliver posing as colossus, threatening to eat annoying Lilliputians, engaging in war, and defending it. The results were unprecedented interpretations of Gulliver as warmonger and ogre (Gillray, pls. 163, 207*, 208; Stephens and George 7: 486 [Ansell], 7: 555 [Cruikshank], 8: 157 [Braddyll], 8: 171 [Charles], 8: 661 [Woodward]).

After 1800, abridgments of *Gulliver's Travels* so eroded Swift's comedy, satire, ideas, and wealth of images that the question was no longer "how can we read the text?" but "what text?" The situation is not altogether different today, thanks to the tradition of Gulliver for children and the consequent comic-book and television versions. There are few literary classics to which students come so thoroughly misled, "knowing" Gulliver without having read the book. Swift asked for it. As many Gulliveriana make clear, he challenged society by taking elements of popular culture as his sources—sailors' memoirs, travel literature in general, the rogue's life, street entertainment, chapbook naïveté, Tom Thumb, Jack the Giant Killer, the lottery mentality, the noble savage—and then mocking these treasured works and attitudes. Society retaliated by creating a metamorphosed Gulliver: mythic, picture-book, once-again-a-hero Gulliver, a man of action, long-suffering, courageous, benevolent, solidly middle-class in values and taste, who after Lilliput settles down with his family, rich and contented. Preconditioned by this happy success story, students may well balk at the real Gulliver. Gulliveriana can be an opening wedge to a new understanding and appreciation.

"Wild" and "Circumstantial" Inventions: Interdisciplinary Possibilities for Teaching *Gulliver's Travels*

Melinda Alliker Rabb

In Robert Hooke's *Micrographia*, there is an enormous engraving of a louse. It unfolds from the pages of the book to a startling length, far exceeding the power of any microscope. In its proportions and in its exploded detail, it assumes a Brobdingnagian mixture of hideousness and magnificence. Why does Hooke's louse have to be so big? I always show my students this engraving during one of the final classes on *Gulliver's Travels*. My reasons for including it and some other visual images are the subject of this essay. Satire can be a difficult genre to teach. Its extravagant fictions—abolishing Christianity, eating babies, worshipping horses—take us on heady flights. Yet, more than any other genre, it binds itself to a real world. It must convince us that the evils it discloses have (or at least had) an existence beyond the text.

Gulliver's Travels justly receives praise for its timeless appeal to the imagination. Its doll-house and gargantuan fantasies, or its fables of immortal and nonhuman life, succeed, according to the Abbé Desfontaines, because of Swift's skill "to make things which are obviously impossible in some way convincing, by deceiving the imagination and seducing his reader's judgment by an arrangement of circumstantial and consecutive inventions . . ." (Williams, *Critical Heritage* 88). But those who teach it frequently are reminded that satire inseparably connects these enduring "inventions" with specific historical figures and events that are all too easily forgotten. Students who know little (or nothing) of Walpole, the Royal Society, or the South Sea Bubble, for example, must read Swift in a radically different way from his contemporaries. To make matters more difficult, a cursory survey of the scholarship surrounding *Gulliver's Travels* implies that a "real understanding" of what informs Gulliver's fantastic voyages would entail mastery of a humbling array of writers and ideas. The list, as various as any Swift devised, might sensibly discourage the most energetic modern reader: Plato, Gelli, Lucian, Hobbes, Locke, Descartes, Fenelon, La Rochefoucauld, St. Augustine, Montaigne, Sprat, Rabelais, de Bergerac, Cervantes, More, Erasmus, Walpole, Harley, Bolingbroke, George I, Dampier, and Ward, to name obvious instances. Most teachers, and certainly most students, would rightly pale in the face of such a task.

Yet Kathleen Williams believes of Swift's original audience that "clearly it was the topical references that first caught the fancy of a period so fascinated by political controversy." To Fielding, Swift becomes "Immortal Swift" because his works "expose and extirpate" specific "Follies and Vices"; "Wit and Humour" earn secondary praise (*Critical Heritage* 110). Voltaire wanted to know all of the historical particulars in *Gulliver's Travels*; otherwise, despite "new fangles, follies of fairytales, of wild inventions, . . . we in France will never have a very good understanding of the books of the ingenious Dr. Swift" (Williams, *Critical Heritage* 94). For our students, these topical references are precisely the least fascinating and accessible part of the work. Does the change in readership also change what the work means? Should we yield to the temptations to teach only the fantasy and it only in relation to our brief minute of history? What is being lost to our students? How much attention can we give to topical references without losing a whole class in a maze of digressions?

To put the problem differently, can we practically teach *Gulliver's Travels* in ways that situate it in details of eighteenth-century life and that explore as well something about satire? I believe the answer is yes, although the method I am proposing may be unorthodox. Images like the giant louse serve as mediators between the facts of Swift's age and the fictions of Swift's satire. A contemporary like Abbé Desfontaines recognized in Gulliver's narrative a synthesis of competing ideals of representation: to represent "above all truth and reality, or at least verisimilitude and possibility," on the one hand, or to represent "fantastic fictions" and "creatures of the fancy," on the other. Swift's friend Arbuthnot also appreciated the interplay within satiric representation by wryly claiming to have "lent the Book [*Gulliver's Travels*] to an Old Gentleman, who went immediately to his Map to search for Lilly put" (Williams, *Critical Heritage* 62). Students cannot and need not duplicate the knowledge or perspective of Arbuthnot and Voltaire. After all, they must imagine "the eighteenth century" just as they must imagine "Lilly put." If they can do both, then Swift's satiric synthesis of historical fact and timeless fiction will work more powerfully on them.

The interdisciplinary approach can coordinate images of diverse origins (from science, philosophy, decorative arts, the popular press, handbooks, etc.) with Swift's text. The kind of image to which I refer is usually a nonsatiric visualization of "facts" that becomes, during class analysis, a metaphor for a way of conceptualizing "facts." Such an image gives observable shape to underlying assumptions about the way human experience is ordered and judged.

Working with material from the late Renaissance to the mid–eighteenth century, I introduce my classes to representations of "truth and reality" from "nonliterary" sources that bear on Swift's "fantastic fictions." Some of these materials may be available at schools with good rare-book libraries. But all of them are available, on request, as slides or as photocopies from libraries in the United States.[1] There are some obvious omissions from my examples, such as the prints of William Hogarth or Hakluyt's *Voyages*, because they have been the subject of extensive study. Sometimes less distinguished works define a norm against which to measure Swift's ironic imagination. Each example must be seen, but I describe the essential imagery of each.

1. Robert Hooke, *Micrographia*: "Of the point of a sharp Needle" (schema 2); "Of fine whaled silk or taffety" (schema 3); "Of the sting of a Bee" (schema 16); "Of a Blue Fly" (schema 26); "Of a Louse (schema 35); title page; "Dedication to the King."

Hooke's *Micrographia*, the title page announces, celebrates the wonders of the microscope and the powers of human observation. Its publication was a scientific event of considerable importance; Hooke was a leading figure in the founding of the Royal Society. *Micrographia* also celebrates other systems of power that shaped the world in which it was produced. Its publication was a statesmanlike political act. The "Dedication to the King" (especially as printed in the first issue) appeals for patronage and alliance with the skillful courtesy of an ambassador. It also marks an economic transaction: the funding of an English academy, as well as the publishing of a book. Finally, it combines a scientific endeavor with a work of art; the handsome engravings, meticulous and even beautiful, implicitly congratulate the Royal Society for its achievements and endorse its methods.

I choose the illustrations that most nearly match the enlarged details described by Gulliver in Brobdingnag, although Hooke's work raises questions pertinent to the other voyages. How might the invention and popularization of the microscope affect the way one conceived of art and nature? Would it increase or decrease one's trust in the powers of human perception? To maintain the scale established by the giant louse, the microscope itself would be as large as a building, and the human observer would be inconceivably tall. Why is Gulliver associated with his spectacles, his pocket perspective, and looking glasses? In his *Micrographia*, Hooke observes that the "[t]op of a small and very sharp Needle . . . seem'd to have been big enough to have afforded a hundred arm'd Mites room enough. . . ." The needle's surface, "though appearing to the naked eye very smooth, could not hide a multitude of holes and scratches and ruggedness from being discover'd." It is interesting to read Hooke's generalizations about nature with Swift in mind. Artificial things prove disappointing to Hooke, but natural objects create greater wonder: "the more we see of [unnatural] *shape*, the less appearance will there be of their *beauty*: whereas in the works of Nature, the deepest Discoveries shew us the greatest Excellencies." As well as episodes from each of Gulliver's voyages, the famous passage from *A Tale of a Tub* comes to mind: "[W]hatever Philosopher or Projector can find an Art to sodder and patch up the Flaws of Nature, will deserve much better of Mankind, and teach . . . a more useful lesson" (Guthkelch and Smith ed. 174).

2. John Wilkins, *Mathematicall Magick: Or, The Wonders That May Be Perform'd by Mechanical Geometry*, p. 81.

Wilkins's curious book is filled with projects based on elaborate systems using wheels, screws, pulleys, and levers. He devotes a chapter (book 2, ch. 6) to "volant automata" or flying objects. The plate to which I refer (book 2, ch. 7; 81) depicts two worlds: one hangs by a pulley; the other balances on a lever. While Hooke's insect is enormous, Wilkins's worlds are tiny and almost barren of detail. They illustrate a chapter titled "Concerning the force of the Mechanick faculties, particularly the Balance and the Lever, How they may be contrived to move the Whole World, or any other conceivable weight." According to Wilkins's mechanical scheme, a child could lift a whole world by the simple movement of a hand. The technical calculations enabling this feat are presented as "Easie . . . Geometrical Truth." But I ask my students to think about it as a fantasy of power that implicitly aggrandizes human intelligence and makes the world its plaything. Wilkins writes: "Thus if we suppose this great Globe A, to contain 2400000000000000000000000 pounds . . . yet a man or Child at D, whose strength perhaps is but equivalent to one hundred, or ten pounds weight, might be able to out weigh and move it." Chapters 18 and 19, on war machines, make clear the application of the kind of power controlled by such mechanical ingenuity. The simplicity and detachment of the visual design will strike most viewers as incongruous with the dramatic claims of the text: namely, that gunpowder may be exploded more effectively and more cheaply by means of "mathematicall Inventions." A puff of gunpowder smoke seems to be the "Magick" Wilkins has in mind. Like Gulliver's description of gunpowder or of the "volant automata" (Laputa), mechanical operations are represented simply, with tempting neatness and objectivity; they thinly mask the messy urges that determine their human applications.

3. "Integrae naturas speculum artisque imago" in Robert Fludd, *Utriusque cosmi historia*. 4. Sir Jonas Moore, *A New System of Mathematicks*, vol. 1. 5. "Der Satyr Silenus."

The first plate of *De macrocosmi historia*, the first volume of Fludd's *Utriusque cosmi historia* (3), represents the order of the universe as conceived by Ptolemy and interpreted by the Renaissance artist. I ask students to explore the relationships between different parts of this all-encompassing "grand plan," particularly the relationships among God, nature, and humankind. Chains (even in black-and-white engraving, one assumes the chains are of gold) connect human beings to nature and nature to God, while circles within circles suggest union and cooperation. It is a harmonious universe, a stable, organized plenitude. Everything from the lowest vegetable to the brightest star has a meaningful place. At the center, humankind is envisioned as the "ape of nature." This conventional emblem connotes nothing satirical to Fludd. The "ape of nature" is rather self-reflective and studious: he sits on top of the earth and holds in one hand a smaller version of the earth, a globe. The compass with which he measures the globe signifies the powers of human reason. (It is useful to show as well the frontispiece to Fludd's *Technica macrocosmi historia*, called "De naturae simia," which elaborates pictorially the ape of nature encircled by all the human arts.)

The frontispiece to *A New System of Mathematicks* alludes to the conceptualization of humanity's rational means of knowledge (or to use Swift's phrase, to the human being as a rational animal) as the "ape of nature." Moore's book, after briefly reviewing basic mathematical functions, is a practical handbook of navigation, such as Gulliver might have read. The frontispiece depicts members of the Royal Society flanking a large globe. In their hands, and on the floor in front of them, are instruments of rational knowledge and measurement: compasses of various kinds, an hourglass, rulers, sequents, charts, and diagrams. One member sits closest to the globe in the precise position of Fludd's "ape of nature" and measures with his compass. A window above opens to a scene of large ships sailing (presumably to carry English trade and knowledge all over the globe), abetted by Neptune and Aeolus. They seem pleased at the idea of English territorial and economic expansion, of commerce aided by science. Finally, two figures in the upper corners reiterate the theme: to the left, a figure with a blank page attends an empty globe stand; the figure on the right bears a compass and a diagram of the hemispheres. Her globe stand is full. The human form has been substituted for the animal image of the earlier visualization of an integrated world, and new political and economic implications are obvious. Moore claims that the use of mathematics "is the great Difference that distinguishes us from Brutes and brutish Men, it changes our Natures, sharpens our Understandings and prepares us for Business."

In contrast, the engraving "Der Satyr Silenus" (1709) satirizes learning in the Royal Society and Oxford. (Pope refers to this print in the *Dunciad* 4.490.) The image of the ape has been borrowed from Fludd but now has been removed from its central position and placed on the floor of a library. The concentric circles have been replaced by the busy and disordered composition of a single room. The compass remains in the ape's hand, but nature's chain and the globe have become a leaden ball and chain attached to the ape's leg. He measures these symbols of his own enslavement to false reason and mistaken knowledge of self and world.

Some questions (of many possibilities) that may ensue from this series of engravings are: What are the implied causes of the disintegration of the Renaissance order? What are the connotations of the adaptations of the "ape of nature" image? Is the monkey episode in book 2 of *Gulliver's Travels* related to the Yahoo encounters of the final book? How does the order of the rational world implied by the engravings compare to the rational world of the Houyhnhnms?

6. Designs from a fan representing Bartholemew Fair (1721), reproduced in Morley 308, 309. Also, "Paye que tombe," or "The English Rope-Dancer" (1697), in *British Museum Catalogue*, no. 1337.

Bartholemew Fair, one of England's long-lived traditions of sanctioned disorder, permitted temporary escape from responsibility. Supposedly, Fielding and Walpole could mingle peacefully in the carnival atmosphere that turned the ordinary into holiday and blurred the usual distinctions between people. The designs reproduced in Morley might be scenes of the court diversions in Lilliput (part 1, ch. 3), but were standard features of the fair. The *Postman* (17 Aug. 1689) advertises "excellent and incomparable performances in Dancing of the Slack Rope, walking on the Slack Rope, Vaulting and Tumbling on the Stage." Other handbills advertise pygmies and giants: "The least Man, Woman, and Horse that ever was seen in the World Alive. The Horse being kept in a box"; "MIRACULA NATURAE; or, a Miracle of Nature, Being that much-admired Gyant-like Young Man . . . of such Prodigious Height and Bigness, . . . that the like hath not been seen in England in the Memory of Man. He was shown of late to his Late and Present Majesties . . . and his Late Majesty was pleased to walk under his Arm, and he is grown very much since."

The fair becomes a metaphor for disorder and confusion. Ropedancing and acrobatics—its real diversions—become more specific metaphors for political power struggles. "The English Rope-Dancer" illustrates a broadside describing the dashed hopes of James II after the Treaty of Ryswick. James II is the principal dancer, but he is blindfolded and is falling off the rope. Other major European dignitaries become the fiddlers, acrobats, drummers, and performers in the scene. The carnival behavior at Bartholemew Fair becomes, in handbills and newspapers, documented historical fact. Conversely, the history of real kings and ministers becomes, for those involved in its real consequences, a bizarre carnival. Swift seems to merge the metaphorical transformation of politics and carnival with the size metaphor.

7. "Vygos Cagados" (1702), in *British Museum Catalogue*, no. 1425.

This frankly unpleasant but memorable broadside is one of many polemical attempts in popular caricature at an "excremental vision." The engraving accounts crudely for "the circumstances which attended and preceeded the victory of Sir G. Rooke, with Dutch and English ships, over the French and Spanish fleets in Vigo Bay." Here "the World's Posteriors" are a metaphor for the waste generated by war and profiteering. Louis XIV is represented explicitly; he is busy rescuing a chest full of money, while hundreds of his French and Spanish supporters perish. A rear-end view of a large ox dominates (in several senses) the entire scene. Wealth, social hierarchy, and political power, as well as the specific battle at Vigo Bay, are "explained" as a series of evacuations. Why does the print lack, or differ from, Swift's scatological power? Is it a difference between pictures and words, or something else? The popular press bitterly attacked enemies. Swift's metaphor for human pride and aggression is not new. Why is it so effective?

In the letter to his cousin Sympson, Gulliver peevishly articulates the dichotomy between "plain Matter of Fact" and "meer Fiction." He complains that "some . . . are so bold as to think my Book of Travels a meer Fiction out of my own Brain." He insists on keeping these categories rigidly apart. But for the reader, Gulliver is the product of their blending, and his prefatory objections ironically enact the satiric synthesis of fact and fantasy. We might say that satire, and *Gulliver's Travels* especially, thrives because "circumstantial" reality and "wild" imagining sometimes look alike.

NOTE

[1]A practical note on how to use these works: All the books I have described are mentioned in the *National Union Catalogue*. The entries in the *Catalogue* list every American library that holds a copy of the work in question. Although it would be difficult to borrow the actual book, it usually is a simple matter to arrange, by phone or letter, for slides or photocopies of relevant pages. Slides have the advantage of enlarged visibility in the classroom, a fair trade for the authenticity of the original rare book.

ASSIGNMENTS

The Use of Dramatic Readings
of *Gulliver's Travels* to Foster Discussion

David J. Leigh

In thirteen years of teaching *Gulliver's Travels* to students from freshman through senior year, I experienced my most exciting class when I first played aloud Alec Guinness's recording of the fourth voyage, chapter 10, on "the author's economy and happy life." The students suddenly began to notice the change in the speaker, his rhetorical shift from utopian description to a ranting list of enemies, and then became aware of the satirical method Swift was using to undercut Gulliver's apparent paradise in Houyhnhnmland. After that time, I always read important passages aloud in class before holding a discussion of them. Eventually I decided to assign one paragraph or passage to small groups of students and let them read them aloud to the class, with the discussion to follow.

The results not only brought the students into active participation but, more importantly, helped them hear for themselves the rhetorical and satiric skill of Swift. As a further consequence, the difficulty of the text seemed to disappear for the students as they became involved in the drama of the story. Thus, a strong pedagogical rationale can be offered for using dramatic readings of key passages of *Gulliver's Travels*: the method brings out the varieties of style, the voices of the characters, the satiric devices, ironies, and contradictions in a manner that involves the students and helps them see and hear for themselves.

A number of preliminary steps are necessary before a teacher assigns student readings, for students are often poor readers or fearful of reading aloud to their classmates. I usually require that the students first read through an entire voyage and learn through lecture or discussion the main historical and narrative background. I also take time to point out simple examples and provide definitions of satire and its more obvious methods: use of irony, exaggeration, inversion, persona, animal imagery, and so on. Since I want to emphasize rhetorical and stylistic strategies, some preliminary explanations and examples are also necessary. Once these preliminaries are over, the following steps have proved helpful:

1. The teacher reads aloud an easy but important passage or uses a recording of such a passage. This formal dramatic reading must be prepared carefully and given with full gusto and nuance. The student may be amazed at the way in which the text comes to life as it leaps off the page through the teacher's dramatization.

2. The teacher gives a close analysis of the passage just read. The analysis may include a description of the speaker (e.g., Gulliver himself, the king of Brobdingnag) at this particular point in the tale. Then the teacher explains how the diction, style, and rhetoric bring out this characterization. The most obvious passages, such as the Lilliputian oath taken by Gulliver in the first voyage, are filled with jargon, inflated sentences, convoluted logic, unnecessary repetition, and other fairly obvious devices. Once they see these elements, the students can give reasons for Swift's use of such style. What is being satirized? How does the very language make fun of it? Thus, the satiric methods and objects are brought out closely together. The teacher can then sum up the method of analysis used: (a) describe the speaker; (b) describe the type of diction, style, and rhetoric used by the speaker; (c) draw conclusions as to what is being satirized, that is, the satiric object; (d) sum up the satiric methods used to ridicule the object; (e) suggest modern persons or situations similar to those satirized in the passage.

3. The teacher assigns approximately three persons to work together on each of a list of passages. One student is to prepare to read the passage aloud in class; the others are to give an analysis of the speaker, style, satiric object, and satiric methods. The students are to work together and practice both the reading and analysis.

4. On an assigned date, the student groups give their dramatic readings and lead a discussion of them in class. The teacher's presentation (and perhaps a method sheet) are to serve as a model for the students' own presentations, although they may often outperform the teacher and lead better discussions. At the end of the discussion, one of the students sums up for the class (perhaps on the board or in

writing for duplication and distribution later) the results of the discussion and analysis.

Since each passage takes about five minutes to be performed, and since a discussion takes fifteen to twenty minutes, my classes usually get through only two such passages in each hour of class. The benefits, however, are such that the use of this method for four consecutive classes—with two passages from each voyage—can bring the entire book to life in a week. I found that students who could not concentrate on the long narrative of Gulliver in the first book and found the opening passage quite dull were suddenly involved when they had to read the first four paragraphs aloud and lead a discussion about the character of Gulliver hidden in that passage. Other students have turned into virtual hams in their performance of the indictment of Gulliver by the Lilliputians in chapter 7 of the first voyage. Gulliver's eulogy of his country leads to a much more powerful undercutting by the king of Brobdingnag at the end of part 2, chapter 6, when the students read aloud the climax: "I cannot but conclude the bulk of your natives to be the most pernicious race of little odious vermin that nature ever suffered to crawl upon the surface of the earth."

Variations might include, along with the readings, the use of student pantomimes, audio- or videotaping, costumes, and music to set the stage. It might even be worth trying the dramatic reading of an entire chapter over a campus radio station. I have found that outstanding students can write modern satirical pieces based on passages in *Gulliver's Travels*, which also lend themselves to dramatic readings.

OTHER PASSAGES FOR DRAMATIC READING

1. 'A letter from Capt. Gulliver to his Cousin Sympson.' Third paragraph ("I do in the next place complain . . . I am wholly a stranger.")
2. Part 1, ch. 3. Articles of liberty ("Golbasto Momaren . . . the ninety-first moon of our reign.")
3. Part 2, ch. 3. Sixth and ninth paragraphs ("His Majesty sent . . . human knowledge." "It was the custom . . . so contemptuously treated.")
4. Part 2, ch. 7. Third to fifth paragraphs ("To confirm . . . politicians put together.")
5. Part 3, ch. 3. Twelfth and thirteenth paragraphs ("If any town . . . to the ground.")
6. Part 3, ch. 6. Final four paragraphs ("I told him . . . home to England.")
7. Part 3, ch. 9. Final four paragraphs ("The dispatch came . . . my wife and family.")
8. Part 4, ch. 1. Fourth paragraph ("In this desolate condition . . . on every side.")

9. Part 4, ch. 4. Final two paragraphs ("I said my birth . . . my own country.")
10. Part 4, ch. 8. Ninth and tenth paragraphs ("As these noble Houyhnhnms . . . superior degree of virtue.")
11. Part 4, ch. 12. Final two paragraphs ("My reconcilement . . . in my sight.")

Gulliver and CAI: "A Project for improving . . . Knowledge by practical and mechanical Operations"

R B Reaves

Computer-assisted instruction (CAI) can help in the study of literature by offering students a tool for exploring a text in preparation for class discussion, lectures, examinations, or essay assignments. Since much of the irony of *Gulliver's Travels* is discovered in the tension between expectation, perception, and reflection, the work requires close reading, which can be reinforced with the exercise outlined in this discussion. My approach to *Gulliver's Travels* encourages students to read the text carefully and to derive their own interpretations within the experience of the work itself without resorting to much information concerning Swift's life and times. My approach is, in short, New Critical, and hardly unusual, I would assume. But such an approach is more easily proposed than accomplished.

An instructor needs to create strategies that will aid students in their reading and their quests for interpretation. I do not suggest that computer technology is essential to teaching the work. The goals that I propose might be achieved through dialogue with students, raising questions that lead to further questions. The real drawback to such an approach is the time involved; CAI technology offers a mechanism for students to explore their ideas before class discussion so that they come not only having read the assignment but also having spent time in serious thought about it.

At first glance it might seem ironic to suggest the application of computer-assisted instruction to teaching a work that ridicules "a Project for improving Speculative Knowledge by practical and mechanical Operations." But this proposal to apply CAI techniques to teaching *Gulliver's Travels* does not promise advancement in learning "without the least Assistance from Genius or Study." Nor is this approach designed to replace the teacher. Properly executed, this exercise prepares the student to explore *Gulliver's Travels* in advance of class discussion or a conference with the teacher.

The exercise described here involves the use of a minicomputer in a system that provides work stations for individual students. The student logs into a directory with a minimum of fifty words available (equivalent to approximately 100K) and calls up the program, which is composed of questions and further questions based upon the student's responses. Students are under no pressure to answer promptly and are in fact encouraged to consider carefully their responses. When the program is completed the student may get a printout as a record of the deliberations, which could be of use for further review or as notes toward a writing assignment. Furthermore, the teacher can get a printout of all responses by all the students, which should provide considerable information concerning how well the class reads as well as the depth and range of understanding and interpretation.

This particular exercise invites the students to imagine that they are playing the role of Gulliver and to answer a number of questions as they think Gulliver would answer them. They will be asked to consider his attributes and characteristics. When these are enumerated, the next stage involves further evaluation and examination. A student, for example, is likely to note that Gulliver is a detailed observer and recorder of what he discovers on his various voyages. The question of reliability of Gulliver's observations is a further probe. The student would be encouraged to compare Gulliver's observations and opinions as they are evident in the first two voyages and then further compare them to those in the last two voyages.

The program can be modified in various ways, but essentially the student does the following steps: the program starts by an opening question to the student impersonating a character, in this case, Gulliver. The student's response is then scanned for at least thirty key words that the instructor has selected. These key words and over one hundred follow-up questions provide the mechanism for probing further. Many questions take the words of the student and incorporate them into a question, after parsing:

COMPUTER.   What do you want to do?

STUDENT.   I want to stay with the Houyhnhnms (horses).

COMPUTER.   Why do you *want to stay with the Houyhnhnms* (horses)?

STUDENT.   Because I believe they are gentle and perfect.

COMPUTER.   Why do you believe that *they are gentle and perfect*?

STUDENT.   I believe they are perfect because they have an ideal society.

COMPUTER.   Why do you believe that *they have an ideal society*?

In the example above the key words are *want* and *believe*. The key words are common words and phrases such as *I think, I want, I feel, why*, *how*, and *when*. The first time a key word is used a specific response is given. The second time, another response is given. The program can be made more complex by adding responses for additional uses of a key word.

One limitation to this program is that the computer can parse only first- and second-person singular constructions:

STUDENT.   I feel that the Houyhnhnms are wonderful creatures.

COMPUTER.   Why do you feel that the Houyhnhnms are wonderful creatures?

The computer can parse "You want" and "You think" constructions as part of the dialogue with the student. But if the student addresses the computer directly the response will redirect the enquiry:

STUDENT.   Why do you not understand?

COMPUTER.   We were discussing you—not me.

The program can also provide a number of general questions that are used when no key word is present in the response, or if the entry is a third-person construction.

STUDENT.   The Houyhnhnms are perfect.

COMPUTER.   Justify what you just said.

"Justify what you just said," "What brings you to this conclusion?" and "Could you give an example?" are three useful general responses. It is probably prudent to limit each of the general responses to only one or two uses. The frequent repetition of one of these general responses can be irritating. The instructor can program many general responses that are essentially variations. The general response "Could you give an example?" might be followed with "Can you provide additional details?" The general responses will not be all that important if the students impersonate Gulliver and respond as if they were experiencing his feelings, his beliefs, and his desires.

The challenge in this program for use with *Gulliver's Travels*, or with almost any work of literature, is in determining the key words for the computer to scan. The next task is to design appropriate questions to respond when a key word is located. The third task is to compose probing questions suitable for a work of satire. With use, the program can be refined, key words added or removed, and both specific and general questions recast. This exercise asks students to raise fundamental questions about *Gulliver's Travels*, and because they are actively involved in exploring Swift's satire they ought to enhance not only their understanding of the work but also their skills as readers of satire and works of irony.

Gulliver's Travels in a Utopias-Dystopias Course

Milton Voigt

Gulliver's Travels fits nicely into a course on utopias and dystopias. The course in question is Great Books—Utopias and Literature. Under our quarter system it runs for ten weeks, meeting three hours per week. Students read one work each week in the following order: Plato, *Republic* (books 1-3, 6-7); More, *Utopia*; Rousseau, *Discourse on Inequality*; Swift, *Gulliver's Travels*; Mill, *On Liberty*; Huxley, *Brave New World*; Skinner, *Walden Two*; Orwell, *1984*. Intervening time is spent reading and discussing selections in the Modern Library anthology *Utopian Literature* (edited by J. W. Johnson), which provides at least a glimpse of utopian writers like Howells and Bellamy and, by way of passages from Bulfinch and Frazer, a chance to consider the golden age and the Saturnalia in their utopian connections.

A formal definition of the genre utopia is rather more easy to come by and to maintain than a definition of dystopia. Instead of spinning out definitions in the abstract, independent of examples, I attempt to use each work as an occasion to define its genre. While Plato did in fact have other and higher aims than elucidating the character and structure of an ideal city-state, the *Republic*'s serious and comprehensive descriptions of the nature and function of producers, guardians, philosopher-kings, and philosopher-queens qualify it nonetheless as a classic utopia, that is, a work in which a better society is described for the reader's approbation and possible imitation. More's work, from which the genre gets its name (Greek for "nowhere," though another etymology yields "well place"), is actually less purely utopian than the *Republic*. The presence of More's own skeptical voice in the work, dissenting from Raphael Hythloday's utopian voice, raises real doubt regarding the classic utopian intention. While Hythloday's discourse, taken by itself without irony, can be safely regarded as utopian, the work as a whole provides an opening for discussion of the second form, dystopia or antiutopia, in which an ostensibly better or at least different society is offered for the reader's consideration but not necessarily for approbation or imitation. The skeptical reservations in the voice to which More gives his own name, along with possibly ironic passages spoken by Hythloday (even his name, Greek for "purveyor of nonsense," undercuts his seriousness), should enable the student to see the ground on which the work might be called antiutopian or dystopian. An example of an unequivocal dystopia will be useful at this point, and I customarily cite Orwell's *1984* (to be read later), which most students already know directly or indirectly. No one seems to doubt that Orwell presents Big Brother and his institutions for our undiluted disapproval.

In the interest of orchestrating a number of thematic relationships, I introduce Rousseau at this point, anachronistically in advance of *Gulliver*. The students read the *Discourse on Inequality* (which some quickly want to label a dystopia), and I extrapolate for them (from *The Social Contract, Emile,* etc.) a picture of Rousseau's ideal society: a Geneva-like city-state (informed with *"Civic* religion") in which individual wills, through a kind of prototototalitarian conditioning, are kept in harmony with the general will, individual and social morality are "natural," and all is harmony and happiness. From the *Discourse on Inequality* they can get a lively sense of the noble savage and Rousseau's championing of spontaneous feeling, along with his version of the state of nature. These themes and concepts are anticipated by Swift (as by Montaigne and others) and are part of the intellectual landscape of *Gulliver's Travels*. A reading of *Gulliver* will be enhanced by some appreciation of Rousseau and his seminal effect on subsequent revolutionary and utopian thought. With the students now in possession of working definitions of utopia and dystopia, and with three major utopias already behind them, we are ready for *Gulliver's Travels* and its utopian-dystopian implications.

First, a few suggestions. The course syllabus or assignment sheet ought to direct the students to postpone reading Gulliver's letter to Sympson until after the last voyage, where it in fact belongs, though all texts print it as prefatory material. I attempt to relieve students' anxieties about topical political and religious references by pointing out that while these were important to Swift and his enemies and friends, they're not what makes the work great, and that "for our purposes" they can be safely left in the shadows where Swift put them.

Some discussion of satire will be needed at this point, and with the help of Frazer on Saturnalia (in J. W. Johnson) I try to explain how reveler-satirists are licensed to perpetrate outrages against established values, how masking and disguise serve these purposes, and how satirists habitually claim to be therapeutic purgers and cleansers of individuals and society. Some examples of satire known to students will be helpful here (Mel Brooks, *National Lampoon, Brave New World*), especially if the examples will illustrate common satirical tricks. I then introduce the distinction between angry and laughing satire, a distinction that everyone seems to know but that few ever think about; scholars have come to label the two styles Juvenalian and Horatian. I alert students to the need to determine the tone of every passage they encounter in *Gulliver* and warn them that in some passages there may be "layers" of tones: one tone in Gulliver's voice, another in the voices Gulliver reproduces for us, still another when the reader senses the inappropriateness or inadequacy of Gulliver's emotional response.

Such preliminaries out of the way, a good place to begin is chapter 6 of part 1, in which students should be able to detect the sudden reversion to the utopian mode, after some preliminary fooling, in paragraph 4. One practice that Gulliver seems to be praising, the rearing of children away from their parents, had been a central feature in the *Republic*, at least among the guardians. For the time being, I prefer to allow these passages, confined to about a dozen paragraphs in chapter 6, to pass unquestioned as utopian, which is what most readers take them to be. One can return to them later after Swift gives further turns to the utopian screw.

Brobdingnag falls considerably short of being ideal, but it has a wise king who directs, tellingly, some righteous indignation against the "bulk" of Gulliver's nation in a passage that overwhelms by sheer force of rhetoric and purity of principle. All the passages involving the Brobdingnagian king (part 2, especially chs. 6-7) are so obviously satiric thrusts against Gulliver's chauvinistic complacency that no one is much tempted to find fault with the king's analyses and values, especially his utopian stand against war and the instruments of war. His righteous indignation ("little odious vermin"), which comes after his avuncular regard for Grildrig (his name for Gulliver), carries the true tone of classic invective—that is, angry satire à la Juvenal, the tone that dominates whenever, in this work, a utopian vision is present.

The third voyage is a mixed bag, not inappropriate in satire, but shifting and diffuse. However, a prevailing dystopian mode is easily recognized by all readers in the abstracted behavior of the Laputan courtiers, in the architectural mayhem, in the experiments of the Grand Academy—all in the tradition of satire directed against absentminded intellectuals and technological bumbling. But the pièce de résistance, as always, will be the Houyhnhnms and their society. A course in utopias and dystopias could not ask for a better conundrum.

Class discussion of the Houyhnhnms and the Yahoos should develop slowly; it is likely to be a succession of reader responses to Gulliver's strange new predicament, the wonderful discoveries, that irrational and unteachable "humans" exist as well as dignified and rational "horses" capable of discourse. Alongside these there is the Houyhnhnms' discovery of Gulliver, their "freak of nature." Students will share Gulliver's wonder at the harmony and serenity of the Houyhnhnms, their freedom from problems, and see all this, rightly, as utopian. This, the common reader's view, can be depended on to emerge in any classroom. Alongside it, however, some dissenting voices will register dissatisfaction with the Houyhnhnms and their society: Is their behavior always so admirable? Are they occasionally laughable? How rational is Gulliver when he identifies with the Houyhnhnms and vilifies Yahoodom? Here emerges the well-known opposition between the two views of the fourth voyage that James L. Clifford has labeled the "hard" and the "soft" schools. I am convinced that Swift wanted both views to be available and tenable, and I take the continued intransigence of the hard and the soft camps to be a sign of Swift's success. Students, of course, will be more open-minded and flexible than our earnest Swift scholars and will be open to the suggestion that the last voyage may be the literary equivalent of trompe l'oeil, especially as practiced by M. C. Escher and other visual tricksters. Perceived the hard-school way, Gulliver has had a vision of perfection, is understandably disenchanted with human nature and human institutions, and, at least for six months or so, mounts the "visionary scheme" of utopian reform. To the soft school, Houyhnhnmland is a put-on, the Houyhnhnms lugubrious in their complacency and earnestness, and Gulliver ultimately a fool in his own little comedy of pretension and pharisaism. The hard view, which perceives Gulliver's Juvenalian anger as pure and correct, will take the conclusion to be utopian. The soft view, with its Horatian detachment from Gulliver and the Houyhnhnms, will see the concluding action as comic and the mode dystopian. In fact, at least two tones are perceivable in the last voyage—Juvenalian anger and Horatian merriment—but these possible responses are separate, not simultaneous. Human perception permits both apprehensions, but not simultaneously. Hence the conclusion of *Gulliver's Travels* is both utopian and dystopian, depending on how it is perceived.

In turn, *Gulliver* becomes part of the context against which the remaining works are read, such as Huxley's satirical dystopia and Skinner's utopian excursion into human engineering. Mill's *On Liberty*, neither a utopia nor a dystopia, is in the course primarily to provide the liberal, bourgeois ideal of freedom of expression and action, not something for which Swift would have had much sympathy. Mill seems remote from Swift and *Gulliver*, but Orwell, not necessarily a kindred spirit, claimed that some of the uglier images in *1984* were inspired by passages in *Gulliver*. (For a discussion of these, see Meyers.) Orwell's stress on the bleak pessimism and despair of *Gulliver* may be yet another abuse of it, but by all signs it seems to thrive on abuse.

A Survey of Writing Assignments on *Gulliver's Travels*

Edward J. Rielly

The survey we conducted in preparation for this volume confirmed that teachers of *Gulliver's Travels* not only try to generate informative and challenging class discussions but also often ask students to respond in writing to the *Travels*. One of the more imaginative of these writing assignments is to ask students to create a partial imitation or a continuation of Swift's book, perhaps a fifth (but inevitably shorter) voyage or an additional episode for part 3. A more modest approach is to ask students to write a satiric account of something to which they object, although not necessarily in strict imitation of Swift's methods. (See Douglas Murray's essay on using this type of assignment with beginning students.)

Many instructors prefer papers that do not involve outside research. They want students to develop their own critical judgment and to engage in close textual analysis and interpretation. One instructor, for example, assigns students a written analysis of a specific passage as a prelude to classroom discussion of irony and persona. Another stirs up controversy by asking students to develop a thesis and a defense of that thesis (in two to three pages) on a matter of contention, such as whether the Houyhnhnms represent an ideal for Swift. A similar assignment is a five-hundred-word essay on such questions as "What is Gulliver's opinion of women?" Another twist to this sort of paper is presented by one instructor who assigns detailed analyses of the text (without outside research) while deliberately guiding students toward topics much discussed by Swift scholars, such as the reasons behind Swift's scatological descriptions in parts 1 and 2. A result of this effort is an interesting comparison between the student's opinion and the judgments of critics, although the teacher must be careful not to give the impression that the student who has a different opinion is somehow not measuring up. Another idea is to have students keep journals in which they record their responses to the *Travels* as they read. (See the concluding paragraph of Smith's essay.) Such candid impressions, in turn, can generate class discussions. These types of assignments clearly testify to the growing popularity of student-response instruction, a matter several essays in this volume address.

Other instructors like to assign research papers of varying lengths to encourage students to sharpen their research skills while also learning more about particular aspects of *Gulliver's Travels*. A variation on this approach is the report on both a critical book and reviews of that book.

The group research project is also useful, and probably more fun for the student than an individual research paper. The instructor may want to have each group present its findings to the whole class, perhaps in a panel-discussion format.

The respondents to our questionnaire suggest a great many topics for papers, including the following: Swift's view of philosophers or scientists; the importance of fantasy in *Gulliver's Travels*; the degree to which the *Travels* is a children's book; Swift's use of irony and persona; similarities and differences between the *Travels* and *Robinson Crusoe* (or another contemporary work); the complementary nature of parts 1 and 2; father and/or mother figures; the relationship between Gulliver and another character; words that Swift repeats (and why he does so); part 4 as another exploration of the big-little contrast; how Gulliver changes within a voyage (or throughout the book); comparisons of Swift's use of big and little with Gay's high and low life in *The Beggar's Opera*; the relationship of *Gulliver's Travels* to seventeenth-century travel books; Swift's use of the *Philosophical Transactions* (or any other source); religious views in the *Travels*; political allegory; sexual allusions and their significance; Swift's use of scatology; the question of misanthropy; whether *Gulliver's Travels* should be considered a novel.

Individual instructors must decide whether a particular topic is suitable for a full-length research paper, a short interpretive essay, a group project, an examination question, or perhaps another type of written assignment. Some of these topics, of course, will also be useful for class discussions.

Teaching *Gulliver's Travels* in Freshman Composition

Robert Keith Miller

At a time when freshman English is widely perceived as a service course, many instructors are increasingly reluctant to use this course as an opportunity for teaching great works of literature. Responding to the need to help students improve basic skills that can no longer be taken for granted, freshman English has become freshman composition, and the prevailing approach to composition is to emphasize reading and writing from "across the curriculum." But instructors do not need to abandon literature altogether. Carefully chosen works of literature can be successfully taught in freshman composition, as long as they generate writing assignments that are closely related to the reading.

Here at Stevens Point, we require two semesters of freshman composition; the first semester focuses on such rhetorical modes as description, process, definition, and classification, while the second concentrates on paraphrase, summary, argument, and research. It has been my experience that *Gulliver's Travels* makes an ideal text during the second half of this sequence. The length and complexity of this work may overwhelm students if they are asked to read it before they have had the chance to gain confidence through less demanding work. But by the second semester of freshman English, most students have had ample experience with short reading assignments and are now ready for longer and more difficult types of reading.

There are plenty of long and difficult texts to choose among, but *Gulliver's Travels* offers several advantages that are not easily matched. Because this work enjoys almost universal recognition as a masterpiece of world literature, students usually perceive it as a book that is worth reading as part of their general education. Because cartoons and other adaptations have made *Gulliver* a myth that transcends the printed page, students feel already familiar with the story and thus approach the work with less anxiety than almost any other eighteenth-century text would inspire. The difficulty of the material is further offset by its fantastic and scatological aspects, which occur regularly enough to encourage reluctant readers. Swift's division of the book into four separate voyages allows for manageable weekly assignments (of one voyage a week), which can be initially treated as self-contained units. Finally, and most important, *Gulliver's Travels* is obviously a work of substance—full of ideas and topics for student essays. As freshmen like to tell me, "This is no book for children!"

Before expecting students to write analytical or argumentative essays on topics drawn from the book, instructors must make sure that students are understanding what they read. Instead of focusing upon the eighteenth-century background to the book, initial class discussion should consider such basic questions as, "Who is Gulliver, and what is he like?" It is important for students to realize that Gulliver is only a character and that he does not always speak for Swift. The first few writing assignments should also be fairly simple, designed principally to test reading comprehension. Students must be able to summarize the book before they can criticize it, and they must be able to paraphrase Swift's prose before they can hope to summarize it. Here are some sample assignments arranged in an order of increasing complexity as the book is read.

Using paraphrase to help students accustom themselves to eighteenth-century prose, instructors can choose any number of key passages as subjects for writing. I recommend allowing twenty to thirty minutes for an in-class paraphrase of a fairly short passage such as the account Gulliver provides of his background in the opening four paragraphs of chapter 1, the terms of the Lilliputian contract with Gulliver in chapter 3, the "Articles of Impeachment" set forth in chapter 7, or the defense Gulliver provides in chapter 6 against the rumor that he had an affair with the treasurer's wife. (This last passage is especially useful since it helps students to see Gulliver's naïveté.) As a follow-up to this exercise, I then ask students to write a paraphrase of a longer passage, such as Gulliver's discussion of English political life with the king of Brobdingnag in chapter 6 of part 2, or the important discussion of warfare in the chapter that follows. This second assignment requires more time, and it is best done out of class.

Similarly, a short summary written in class can help prepare students for a more complex assignment involving both summary and synthesis. I ask students to write a paragraph-long summary on such topics as Lilliputian government, Gulliver's adventures with animals in Brobdingnag, the experiments conducted at the Grand Academy of Lagado, the view of history presented during Gulliver's visit to Glubbdubdrib, and the way Struldbruggs spend their lives. A subsequent out-of-class assignment can help students understand Gulliver's third voyage, which is the part of the book that causes them the most difficulty: "Summarize Gulliver's adventures in part 3 and determine whether they have anything in common."

By the time they reach "A Voyage to the Land of the Houyhnhnms," students are usually ready to attempt an analytical essay that will require writing with a thesis. Because the first several writing assignments on the book have been very specific, I encourage students to choose their own topics for this paper. But because some students find it difficult to do so, I also provide some suggestions: "Do the Houyhnhnms have an ideal society? Would you like to live in a world governed by their principles?" "What are we meant to learn from the example of Don Pedro, the Portuguese sea captain?" "Are Yahoos human?" "What is Swift's opinion of women?" "Does Gulliver make any mistakes?" "Does Swift ever seem to contradict himself?"

Because I teach other works in the course, I do not require students to write a research paper on *Gulliver's Travels*, but I do provide students with this option. I also encourage papers that will involve research on some aspect of eighteenth-century society that has been touched on in the book. Among the possibilities are papers on eighteenth-century science, philosophy, and exploration, as well as papers on English political history and religious conflict. A few students choose to read literary criticism, but this is something I would never insist on with freshmen in a required course.

Instructors of freshman composition cannot assume that students already possess the skills that these assignments require. The emphasis of the course must be on the acquisition of these skills. Because freshman English should help prepare students for the many different types of work that will be expected of them in college, instructors should include reading from a variety of disciplines, and *Gulliver* should be taught as only one of several texts in the course. But teachers teach best when they are teaching material they care about. Anyone who enjoys *Gulliver* should consider experimenting with it in freshman composition. It can help students become more sophisticated readers and supply them with abundant material for writing. More important, it is a book that makes students think, and, we must not forget, thinking is the beginning and end of writing.

Writing a Satire: Or, Everyone His or Her Own Swift

Douglas Murray

I take the following passage from James Moffett's *Active Voice* as my epigraph:

> When I assign a topic such as "loyalty" or "Irony in A. E. Housman," all I am asking the student to do is to find illustrations for my classifications. By doing half of his work for him, I am impoverishing his education. Rather than assign literary exegesis, I would have him write in the forms he reads. As practitioner he will naturally be a better literary critic than a student who only analyzes. (147)

While I and most other teachers of literature do not share Moffett's distrust of literary exegesis, I do share his belief that students can become actively engaged in reading literature by creating the sort of works that they study in class. But while they can read *Hamlet* or *Othello*, few students have the time, experience, and skill needed to write a tragedy. One genre that students can successfully produce, however, is satire. I have found that the same college freshmen and sophomores who would feel self-conscious creating a modern version of a Shakespearean sonnet can, while studying *Gulliver's Travels*, write good satire. Most have a sense of humor and appreciate the absurd; despite the reigning conservatism of our decade, most of them are beginning to become amused and angry at some ludicrousness in the adult world.

If students are to write satires, it is helpful first to convince them of the continued existence and, indeed, health of the satiric impulse. Hence, I sometimes accompany my initial discussion and definition of satire with contemporary examples, usually in the form of spiky political cartoons. Students decide what is being attacked in each cartoon—the satiric target—and the means by which the artist's judgments become manifest—the satiric technique. I sometimes introduce contemporary prose satire: I am especially fond of Cathleen Schine's "Seek Dwellings for MX." Then the class turns to part 1 of *Gulliver*, and many of the techniques Swift uses there are already familiar, for chances are that students have met in the cartoons something of that which Gulliver encounters in Lilliput—those same comic physical exaggerations and those belittling reductions of what one usually sees as "serious" situations.

After viewing and reading satire, students can then write their own. I find it necessary to emphasize that students are producing *satires*, not just funny and absurd stories; there must be a satiric target that the reasonably attentive reader will pick up on. I also emphasize that satire works by indirection and nuance and hence is no place for the direct criticism characteristic of nonfiction essays. Since Swift presents *Gulliver* in the form of a mock travel book, I tell students that they might couch their satires in some mock form—a mock holy book (the Ten Commandments as revised for and specially revealed to yuppies), a mock course description, a mock script for an advertisement, or a mock etiquette lesson. Swift frequently makes Gulliver into an ingenue who does not understand the implications of what he describes, so I suggest that students too might adopt the point of view of the ignorant and guileless bumpkin confronted with whatever their satire targets. Since Gulliver is a traveler, I suggest that they imagine they are seeing some part of American culture from a radically new perspective—through the eyes of a non-Westerner, of a medieval person, or of a visitor from the twenty-second century.

Students then become satirists, some of them very good ones, some of them seeing more objectively the principles and customs on which they have hitherto based their lives. They are proud of their own works and enjoy reading one another's. So that everyone's essay gets some exposure, I have encouraged and sometimes required classmates to read one another's satires in pairs or small groups. In guiding the readers' responses, I distribute the following questions: What is the author's satiric target? Exactly where in the paper does the target become clear? How does the author communicate his criticism? What are the satiric techniques? What is the author's tone—gentle criticism, harsh rebuke, or something in between? Does the author ever resort to direct criticism?

I do not see this sort of assignment as an end in itself, though the production of telling satire is by no means a contemptible achievement. Rather, I find that students, after having adopted the satirist's perspective, can better read Swift's masterpiece and other satiric works. They are familiar with the principle of indirection, so they are not likely to be stymied by *A Modest Proposal*. They know about mock forms, so they can quickly understand the mock epic of *The Rape of the Lock*.

And, of course, after writing their own satires, students are prepared to write analysis. I encourage them to take a brief portion of *Gulliver* —a paragraph or a unified but short episode—and ask themselves the following by-now familiar questions about it: What is the chief satiric target there? By what indirect means does Swift make his criticism known? What is the author's submerged tone toward his subject matter? Students are now ready to answer such exegetical questions with sophistication; novices in literary criticism *can* then write the sort of analytical essays that Moffett disparages but that most instructors ultimately require.

I do not see this sort of preliminary satiric essay as suitable for all students. Upper-level undergraduates are beyond it. But those freshmen and sophomores lucky enough to be assigned *Gulliver* will find writing their own satires an excellent introduction to Swift's art. And they will have a chance to learn that literature and life are not as separate as most of them think, that great authors have experienced an indignation and amusement like their own, and that it is possible to convert such criticism, whether savage or gentle, into art.

PARTICIPANTS IN SURVEY OF
GULLIVER'S TRAVELS
INSTRUCTORS

The following scholars and teachers generously agreed to participate in the survey of approaches to teaching *Gulliver's Travels* that preceded the preparation of this volume. Without their invaluable assistance and support, the volume simply would not have been possible.

Janet E. Aikins, Univ. of New Hampshire; Mary Lee Archer, Victoria Coll.; Jack M. Armistead, Univ. of Tennessee, Knoxville; Paula R. Backscheider, Univ. of Rochester; Louise K. Barnett, Rutgers Univ., New Brunswick; Donald A. Bloom, Davis and Elkins Coll.; Gisela Casines, Florida International Univ.; Brian Corman, Univ. of Toronto; Kenneth Craven, New Providence, NJ; Michael DePorte, Univ. of New Hampshire; Ann W. Engar, Univ. of Utah; Christopher Fox, Univ. of Notre Dame; Sidney Gottlieb, Sacred Heart Univ.; Mark L. Greenberg, Drexel Univ.; Sally Hand, William Paterson Coll.; Charles H. Hinnant, Univ. of Missouri, Columbia; Nora Crow Jaffe, Smith Coll.; Edward Jennings, State Univ. of New York, Albany; Ann Kelly, Howard Univ.; Deborah J. Knuth, Colgate Univ.; David J. Leigh, Seattle Univ.; Roger D. Lund, Le Moyne Coll.; Robert Keith Miller, Univ. of Wisconsin, Stevens Point; Douglas Murray, Belmont Coll.; Leonard Mustazza, Pennsylvania State Univ., Ogontz; Dolores Palomo, Univ. of Washington; R. G. Peterson, St. Olaf Coll.; Irwin Primer, Rutgers Univ., Newark; Charles H. Pullen, Queen's Univ.; Melinda Alliker Rabb, Brown Univ.; Claude Rawson, Univ. of Warwick; R B Reaves, Univ. of Rhode Island; Blakeney Richard, Texas A&I Univ.; Edward J. Rielly, Saint Joseph's Coll., Maine; Richard H. Rodino, Holy Cross Coll.; Deborah Rogers, Univ. of Maine, Orono; Edward C. Sampson, State Univ. of New York, Oneonta; Paul Sawyer, Bradley Univ.; Peter J. Schakel, Hope Coll.; John F. Sena, Ohio State Univ., Columbus; Frederik N. Smith, Univ. of North Carolina, Charlotte; Ann Straulman, Univ. of Western Ontario; Charles Trainor, Siena Coll.; David K. Vaughan, Univ. of Maine, Orono; Milton Voigt, Univ. of Utah; Gene Washington, Utah State Univ.; Howard Weinbrot, Univ. of Wisconsin, Madison; Jeanne K. Welcher, Long Island Univ., C. W. Post Center

WORKS CITED

Adams Percy G. *Travellers and Travel Liars 1660-1800*. Berkeley: U of California P, 1962.

Allison, Alexander W. "Concerning Houyhnhnm Reason." *Sewanee Review* 76 (1968): 480-92.

Argyle, Michael. *Bodily Communication*. London: IUP, 1975.

——. *Gaze and Mutual Gaze*. Cambridge: Cambridge UP, 1976.

——. *Social Interaction*. New York: Atherton, 1969.

Ashley, Maurice. *England in the Seventeenth Century*. 3rd ed. Pelican History of England 6. Baltimore: Penguin, 1966.

Beauchamp, Gorman. "Gulliver's Return to the Cave: Plato's *Republic* and Book IV of *Gulliver's Travels*." *Michigan Academician* 7 (1974): 201-09.

Beckett, J. C. "Swift and the Anglo-Irish Tradition." Rawson, *Focus* 155-70.

Bentman, Raymond. "Satiric Structure and Tone in the Conclusion of *Gulliver's Travels*." *Studies in English Literature, 1500-1900* 11 (1971): 535-48.

Bergson, Henri. "Laughter" (1900). Rpt. in *Comedy*. Intro and appendix by Wylie Sypher. Garden City: Doubleday, 1956. 59-190.

Bonner, William Hallam. *Captain Dampier: Buccaneer-Author*. Stanford: Stanford UP, 1934.

Bony, Alain. " 'Call Me Gulliver.' " *Poétique* 14 (1973): 197-209.

Booth, Wayne C. *The Rhetoric of Fiction*. Chicago: U of Chicago P, 1961.

Boswell, James. *Life of Johnson*. 1791. Ed. G. B. Hill and L. F. Powell. Oxford: Clarendon, 1934.

Boyce, Benjamin. "News from Hell: Satiric Communications with the Nether World in English Writing of the Seventeenth and Eighteenth Centuries." *PMLA* 58 (1943): 402-37.

Bracher, Frederick. "The Maps in *Gulliver's Travels*." *Huntington Library Quarterly* 8 (1944-45): 59-74.

Brady, Frank, ed. *Twentieth Century Interpretations of* Gulliver's Travels: *A Collection of Critical Essays*. Englewood Cliffs: Prentice, 1968.

——. "Vexations and Diversions: Three Problems in *Gulliver's Travels*." *Modern Philology* 75 (1978): 346-67.

Brengle, Richard L. "Very Knowing Americans: Jonathan Swift and America: His Reputation and Influence, 1720-1860." Diss. Columbia U, 1962.

Brink, J. R. "From the Utopians to the Yahoos: Thomas More and Jonathan Swift." *Journal of the Rutgers University Libraries* 42 (1980): 59-66.

Brown, Norman. "The Excremental Vision." *Life against Death*. Middletown: Wesleyan UP, 1959. 179-201.

Bullitt, John. *Jonathan Swift and the Anatomy of Satire.* Cambridge: Harvard UP, 1953.

Carnochan, W. B. "The Complexity of Swift: Gulliver's Fourth Voyage." *Studies in Philology* 60 (1963): 23-44.

———. *Lemuel Gulliver's Mirror for Man.* Berkeley: U of California P, 1968.

Case, Arthur. *Four Essays on* Gulliver's Travels. Princeton: Princeton UP, 1945.

Castle, Terry J. "Why the Houyhnhnms Don't Write: Swift, Satire and the Fear of the Text." *Essays in Literature* 7 (1980): 31-44.

Champion, Larry S., ed. *Quick Springs of Sense: Studies in the Eighteenth Century.* Athens: U of Georgia P, 1974.

Clifford, James L. "Argument and Understanding: Teaching through Controversy." *Eighteenth-Century Life* 5.3 (1979): 1-7.

———. "Gulliver's Fourth Voyage: 'Hard' and 'Soft' Schools of Interpretation." Champion 33-49.

Clubb, Merrell D. "The Criticism of Gulliver's 'Voyage to the Houyhnhnms,' 1726-1914." *Stanford Studies in Language and Literature: Fiftieth Anniversary of the Founding of Stanford University.* Ed. Hardin Craig. Palo Alto: Stanford UP, 1941. 203-32.

Cohan, Steven M. "Gulliver's Fiction." *Studies in the Novel* 6 (1974): 7-16.

Cook, Terry. " 'Dividing the Swift Mind': A Reading of *Gulliver's Travels.*" *Critical Quarterly* 22 (1980): 35-47.

Crane, R. S. "The Houyhnhnms, the Yahoos, and the History of Ideas." *Reason and the Imagination: Studies in the History of Ideas.* Ed. J. A. Mazzeo. New York: Columbia UP, 1962. 231-53. Rpt. in Swift, *Gulliver's Travels* (ed. Greenberg) 402-06.

———. "The Rationale of the Fourth Voyage." Swift, *Gulliver's Travels* (ed. Greenberg) 331-38.

Culler, Jonathan. *Structuralist Poetics: Structuralism, Linguistics, and the Study of Literature.* Ithaca: Cornell UP, 1975.

Dampier, William. *A New Voyage round the World.* London, 1691.

———. *A Voyage to New Holland, &c.* 1699. Ed. James Spencer. Gloucester: Sutton, 1981.

Dennis, Nigel. *Jonathan Swift.* New York: Macmillan, 1964.

Dobrée, Bonamy. *English Literature in the Early Eighteenth Century.* Oxford: Clarendon, 1959.

Donoghue, Denis, ed. *Jonathan Swift: A Critical Anthology.* Baltimore: Penguin, 1971.

Dryden, John. *"Of Dramatic Poesy" and Other Critical Essays.* Ed. George Watson. 2 vols. London: Dent, 1962.

Duthie, Elizabeth. "Gulliver Art." *Scriblerian* 10 (1978): 127-31.

Dyson, A. E. "Swift: The Metamorphosis of Irony." *Essays and Studies* 11 (1958): 53-67.

Easthope, A. K. "The Disappearance of Gulliver: Character and Persona at the End of the 'Travels.'" *Southern Review* (Adelaide) 2 (1967): 261-66.

Eddy, William A. *On Gulliver's Travels: A Critical Study*. Princeton: Princeton UP, 1923.

Ehrenpreis, Irvin. "The Meaning of Gulliver's Last Voyage." *Review of English Literature* 3.3 (1962): 18-38.

———. "The Origins of *Gulliver's Travels*." Jeffares 200-25.

———. *The Personality of Jonathan Swift*. Cambridge: Harvard UP, 1958.

———. *Swift: The Man, His Works, and the Age*. 3 vols. Cambridge: Harvard UP, 1962-83.

———. "Swift's Letters." Rawson, *Focus* 197-215.

Ferguson, Oliver. *Jonathan Swift and Ireland*. Champaign: U of Illinois P, 1962.

Fetrow, Fred M. "Swift's *Gulliver's Travels*." *Explicator* 35.3 (1977): 29-31.

Fish, Stanley. *Is There a Text in This Class? The Authority of Interpretive Communities*. Cambridge: Harvard UP, 1980.

Fitzgerald, Robert P. "The Structure of *Gulliver's Travels*." *Studies in Philology* 71 (1974): 247-63.

Fludd, Robert. *Utriusque cosmi historia*. 2 vols. London, 1617-19.

Foster, Milton P., ed. *A Casebook on Gulliver among the Houyhnhnms*. New York: Crowell, 1961.

Fox, Christopher. "The Myth of Narcissus in Swift's *Travels*." *Eighteenth-Century Studies* 20 (1986): 17-33.

Frantz, R. W. *The English Traveller and the Movement of Ideas, 1660-1732*. Lincoln: U of Nebraska P, 1934.

Freud, Sigmund. *Wit and Its Relation to the Unconscious*. Trans. A. A. Brill. 2nd ed. New York: Moffat, 1917.

Frye, Roland. "Swift's Yahoo and the Christian Symbols for Sin." *Journal of the History of Ideas* 15 (1954): 201-17.

Fussell, Paul. *The Rhetorical World of Augustan Humanism*. Oxford: Clarendon, 1965.

George, Dorothy. *London Life in the Eighteenth Century*. New York: Capricorn, 1965.

Gill, James E. "Beast over Man: Theriophilic Paradox in Gulliver's 'Voyage to the Country of the Houyhnhnms.'" *Studies in Philology* 67 (1970): 532-49.

———. "Man and Yahoo: Dialectic and Symbolism in Gulliver's 'Voyage to the Country of the Houyhnhnms.'" *The Dress of Words: Essays on Restoration and Eighteenth Century Literature in Honor of Richmond P. Bond*. Ed. Robert B. White, Jr. U of Kansas Publications, Library Series 42. Lawrence: U of Kansas Libraries, 1978. 67-90.

Gillray, James. *Works of James Gillray*. 1851. New York: Blom, 1968.

Goldgar, Bertrand. *Walpole and the Wits: The Relation of Politics to Literature*. Lincoln: U of Nebraska P, 1976.

Goldin, Frederick. *The Mirror of Narcissus in the Courtly Love Lyric*. Ithaca: Cornell UP, 1967.

Gosse, Edmund. *A History of Eighteenth-Century Literature*. New York, 1889.

Goulding, Sybil. *Swift en France*. Paris: Bibliothéque de la Revue de Littérature Comparée, 1924.

Gove, Philip Babcock. *The Imaginary Voyage in Prose Fiction . . . with an Annotated Checklist*. 1941. London: Holland, 1961.

Gravil, Richard, ed. *Swift: Gulliver's Travels: A Casebook*. London: Macmillan, 1974.

Greene, Donald. *The Age of Exuberance: Backgrounds to Eighteenth-Century English Literature*. New York: Random, 1970.

———. "The Education of Lemuel Gulliver." *The Varied Pattern: Studies in the Eighteenth Century*. Ed. Peter Hughes and David Williams. Toronto: Hakkert, 1971. 3-20.

———. "The Sin of Pride: A Sketch for a Literary Exploration." *New Mexico Quarterly* 34 (1964): 8-30.

Guinness, Alec. *Alec Guinness Reads Jonathan Swift, including Selections from* Gulliver's Travels. Prod. Jean Stein. Loews Arcady Ser. E3620 ARC, n.d.

Gulliveriana I-VI. Introd. J. K. Welcher and George E. Bush, Jr. Delmar, NY: Scholars' Facsimiles and Reprints, 1970-76. Forthcoming, *Gulliveriana VII*. Ed. J. K. Welcher. Delmar: Scholars' Facsimiles. (An annotated list of all known eighteenth-century Gulliveriana, with topical appendixes, index to vols. 1-7, and reproductions of Gulliverian artworks.)

Halewood, William H. "Plutarch in Houyhnhnmland: A Neglected Source for Gulliver's Fourth Voyage." *Philological Quarterly* 44 (1965): 185-94.

Halewood, William H., and Marvin Levich. "Houyhnhnm est animal rationale." *Journal of the History of Ideas* 26 (1965): 273-81.

Harth, Phillip, ed. *New Approaches to Eighteenth-Century Literature: Selected Papers from the English Institute*. New York: Columbia UP, 1974.

———. "The Problem of Political Allegory in *Gulliver's Travels*." *Modern Philology* 73 (1976): S40-S47.

———. *Swift and Anglican Rationalism*. Chicago: U of Chicago P, 1961.

Hassall, Anthony J. "Discontinuities in *Gulliver's Travels*." *Sydney Studies in English* 5 (1979-80): 3-14.

Hobbes, Thomas. *Leviathan*. 1651. London: Dent; New York: Dutton, 1965.

Hogarth, William. *Hogarth's Graphic Works*. Ed. and rev. Ronald Paulson. New Haven: Yale UP, 1970.

Holly, Grant. "Travel and Translation: Textuality in *Gulliver's Travels*." *Criticism* 21 (1979): 134-52.

Holmes, Geoffrey Shorter. *British Politics in the Age of Anne*. New York: St. Martin's; London: Macmillan, 1967.

Hooke, Robert. *Micrographia*. London, 1665.

Huxley, Aldous. *Brave New World*. 1932. New York: Harper, 1969.

Ingarden, Roman. *The Cognition of the Literary Work of Art*. Trans. Ruth Ann Crowley and Kenneth R. Olson. Evanston: Northwestern UP, 1973.

Iser, Wolfgang. *The Act of Reading: A Theory of Aesthetic Response*. Baltimore: Johns Hopkins UP, 1978.

——. *The Implied Reader: Patterns of Communication in Prose Fiction from Bunyan to Beckett*. Baltimore: Johns Hopkins UP, 1974.

Jeffares, A. Norman, ed. *Fair Liberty Was All His Cry: A Tercentenary Tribute to Jonathan Swift, 1667-1745*. London: Macmillan; New York: St. Martin's, 1967.

Johnson, J. W., ed. *Utopian Literature*. New York: Modern Library, 1968.

Johnson, Samuel. "Debates in the Senate of Lilliput." *Gentleman's Magazine, 1738-46*. Ed. Benjamin B. Hoover. New Haven: Yale UP, forthcoming. Vols. 11-13 in the Yale *Works of Samuel Johnson*.

Jones, Richard Foster. *Ancients and Moderns: A Study of the Rise of the Scientific Movement in Seventeenth-Century England*. 2nd ed. St. Louis: Washington UP, 1961.

Kallich, Martin. *The Other End of the Egg: Religious Satire in* Gulliver's Travels. Bridgeport, CT: Conference on British Studies at the U of Bridgeport, 1970.

Karl, Frederick R. *A Reader's Guide to the Eighteenth-Century English Novel*. New York: Farrar, 1974.

Keener, Frederick M. *English Dialogues of the Dead*. New York: Columbia UP, 1973.

Keesey, Donald. "The Distorted Image: Swift's Yahoos and the Critics." *Papers on Language and Literature* 15 (1979): 320-32.

Kelling, H. D. "*Gulliver's Travels IV*, Once More." *Scholia Satyrica* 2.2 (1976): 3-12.

Kelly, Ann Cline. "Swift's Explorations of Slavery in Houyhnhnmland and Ireland." *PMLA* 91 (1976): 846-55.

Kelsall, M. M. "*Iterum* Houyhnhnm: Swift's Sextumvirate and the Horses." *Essays in Criticism* 19 (1969): 35-45.

Kenner, Hugh. *The Stoic Comedians*. Berkeley: U of California P, 1962.

Kenyon, J. P. *Stuart England*. New York: Penguin, 1978.

Kinsley, William. "Gentle Readings: Recent Work in Swift." *Eighteenth-Century Studies* 15 (1981-82): 442-53.

Knowles, A. S., Jr. "Defoe, Swift, and Fielding: Notes on the Retirement Theme." *Champion* 121-36.

Korshin, Paul. "The Intellectual Context of Swift's Flying Island." *Philological Quarterly* 50 (1971): 630-46.

Kramnick, Isaac. *Bolingbroke and His Circle*. Cambridge: Harvard UP, 1968.

LaCasce, Steward. "The Fall of Gulliver's Master." *Essays in Criticism* 20 (1970): 327-33.

——. "Gulliver's Fourth Voyage: A New Look at the Critical Debate." *Satire Newsletter* 8.1 (1970): 5-7.

La Fontaine, Jean de. "The Man and His Reflection." *The Fables of La Fontaine*. Trans. Marianne Moore. New York: Viking, 1952. 22–23.

Landa, Louis. "The Dismal Science in Houyhnhnmland." *Novel* 13 (1979): 38-49.

———. *Swift and the Church of Ireland*. Oxford: Clarendon, 1954.

Landa, Louis, and J. E. Tobin. *Jonathan Swift: A List of Critical Studies Published from 1895 to 1945*. New York: Cosmopolitan Science and Art Service, 1945.

Leavis, F. R. *The Common Pursuit*. New York: Stewart, 1952.

Leigh, Jon S. "Dr. Lemuel Gulliver and 'The Thing Which Was Not.'" *Philosophy and Literature* 4 (1980): 92-106.

Lenfest, David S. "A Checklist of Illustrated Editions of *Gulliver's Travels*, 1727-1914." *Papers of the Bibliographical Society of America* 62 (1968): 85-123.

———. "LeFebvre's Illustrations of *Gulliver's Travels*." *New York Public Library Bulletin* 76 (1972): 199-208.

Leyburn, Ellen Douglass. *Satiric Allegory: Mirror for Man*. New Haven: Yale UP, 1956.

Lock, F. P. *The Politics of* Gulliver's Travels. Oxford: Clarendon, 1980.

Lovejoy, Arthur. *The Great Chain of Being*. 1936. New York: Harper & Row, 1960.

Mack, Maynard. "*Gulliver's Travels*." Tuveson, *Swift* 111-14.

"The Majestic Clockwork." Writ. J. Bronowski. *The Ascent of Man*. Created, writ., and dir. J. Bronowski. Prod. Richard Gilling. Series ed. Adrian Malone. BBC. 1973.

Malraux, André. *Saturn: An Essay on Goya*. London: Phaidon, 1957.

[Mandeville, Bernard.] *A Modest Defence of Publick Stews*. London, 1724. Los Angeles: Clark Library, Augustan Reprint Soc., 1973.

McManmon, John J. "The Problem of a Religious Interpretation of Gulliver's Fourth Voyage." *Journal of the History of Ideas* 27 (1966): 59-72.

Merton, Robert C. "The 'Motionless' Motion of Swift's Flying Island." *Journal of the History of Ideas* 27 (1966): 275-77.

Meyers, Jeffrey. *A Reader's Guide to George Orwell*. 1975. Totowa, NJ: Littlefield, 1977.

Mezciems, Jenny. "The Unity of Swift's 'Voyage to Laputa': Structure as Meaning in Utopian Fiction." *Modern Language Review* 72 (1977): 1-21.

Mill, John Stuart. *On Liberty*. Harmondsworth: Penguin, 1974.

Milton, John. *Complete Poems and Major Prose*. Ed. Merritt Y. Hughes. Indianapolis: Odyssey, 1957.

Moffett, James. *Active Voice: A Writing Program across the Curriculum*. New York: Boynton, 1981.

Monk, Samuel Holt. "The Pride of Lemuel Gulliver." *Sewanee Review* 63 (1955): 48-71. Rpt. in Swift, *Gulliver's Travels* (ed. Greenberg) 312-30.

Moore, Cecil A. "The English Malady." *Backgrounds of English Literature: 1700-1760*. Minneapolis: U of Minnesota P, 1953. 179-235.

Moore, John B. "The Role of Gulliver." *Modern Philology* 25 (1928): 469-80.

Moore, Sir Jonas. *A New System of Mathematicks*. London, 1681.

More, Thomas. *Utopia*. 1516. Trans. and ed. Robert M. Adams. New York: Norton, 1975.

Morley, Henry. *Memoirs of Bartholemew Fair*. London, 1859.

Morris, Desmond. *Gestures: Their Origin and Distribution*. New York: Stein, 1979.

Morris, John. "Wishes as Horses: A Word for the Houyhnhnms." *Yale Review* 62 (1972-73): 354-71.

Munro, John. "Book III of *Gulliver's Travels* Once More." *English Studies* 49 (1968): 429-36.

Nicolson, Marjorie. *Science and Imagination*. Ithaca: Cornell UP, 1956.

Nicolson, Marjorie, and Nora M. Mohler. "The Scientific Background of Swift's *Voyage to Laputa*." *Annals of Science* 2 (1937): 299-334. Rpt. in Jeffares 226-69.

Nokes, David. *Jonathan Swift, a Hypocrite Reversed: A Critical Biography*. New York: Oxford UP, 1985.

Nordon, Pierre. "L'effet de glissement dans *Gulliver's Travels*." *Langues Modernes* 62 (1968): 496-99.

Novak, Maximilian E. "The Wild Man Comes to Tea." *The Wild Man Within*. Ed. Edward Dudley and Maximilian E. Novak. Pittsburgh: U of Pittsburgh P, 1972. 183-221.

Oakleaf, David. "*Trompe l'Oeil*: Gulliver and the Distortions of the Observing Eye." *University of Toronto Quarterly* 53 (1983-84): 166-80.

Onania: or, The Heinous Sin of Self-Pollution, and All Its Frightful Consequences. London, 1725.

Otten, Robert M. "Lemuel Gulliver, Projector." *Notre Dame English Journal* 5.1 (1969-70): 5-15.

Ovid. *Metamorphoses*. Trans. F. J. Miller. Cambridge: Harvard UP, 1936.

Peake, Charles. "The Coherence of *Gulliver's Travels*." Rawson, *Focus* 171-96.

———. "Swift and the Passions." *Modern Language Review* 15 (1960): 169-80.

Phillipson, John S. "Swift's Half-Way House." *Medical History* 13 (1969): 297-98.

Philmus, Robert M. "The Language of Utopia." *Studies in the Literary Imagination* 6.2 (1973): 61-78.

———. "Swift, Gulliver, and 'The Thing Which Was Not.'" *English Literary History* 38 (1971): 62-79.

Philosophical Transactions of the Royal Society of London. 177 vols. London, 1665/66–1886. Vols. 16, 25, 26, 27.

Pierre, Gerald J. "Gulliver's Voyage to China and Moor Park: The Influence of Sir William Temple upon *Gulliver's Travels*." *Texas Studies in Literature and Language* 17 (1975): 427-37.

Plumb, J. H. *England in the Eighteenth Century (1714-1815)*. Pelican History of England 7. 1950. Baltimore: Penguin, 1966.

Porter, Roy. *English Society in the Eighteenth Century*. Pelican Social History of Britain. New York: Penguin, 1983.

Probyn, Clive T. *The Art of Jonathan Swift*. London: Vision, 1978.

————, ed. *Jonathan Swift: The Contemporary Background*. New York: Harper, 1979.

————. "Man, Horse and Drill: Temple's *Essay on Popular Discontents* and Gulliver's Fourth Voyage." *English Studies* 55 (1974): 358-60.

————. *The Art of Jonathan Swift*. London: Vision, 1978.

Pullen, Charles H. "Gulliver: Student of Nature." *Dalhousie Review* 51 (1971): 77-89.

Pyle, Fitzroy. "Yahoo: Swift and the Asses." *Ariel* 3.2 (1972): 64-69.

Quinlan, Maurice J. "Treason in Lilliput." *Texas Studies in Literature and Language* 11 (1970): 1317-32.

Quintana, Ricardo. "*Gulliver's Travels*: The Satiric Intent and Execution." *Jonathan Swift, 1667-1967: A Dublin Tercentenary Tribute*. Ed. Roger McHugh and Philip Edwards. Dublin: Dolmen; London: Oxford UP, 1967. 78-93.

————. *The Mind and Art of Jonathan Swift*. New York: Oxford UP, 1936.

————. "Situational Satire: A Commentary on the Method of Swift." *University of Toronto Quarterly* 17 (1948): 130-36.

————. *Swift: An Introduction*. London: Oxford UP, 1955.

Rabkin, Eric. *The Fantastic in Literature*. Princeton: Princeton UP, 1976.

Rader, Ralph W. "Fact, Theory, and Literary Explanation." *Critical Inquiry* 1 (1974): 245-72.

Radner, John B. "The Struldbruggs, the Houyhnhnms, and the Good Life." *Studies in English Literature* 17 (1977): 419-33.

Rawson, C. J. *The Character of Swift's Satire*. Newark: U of Delaware P, 1983.

————, ed. *Focus: Swift*. London: Sphere, 1971.

————. "Gulliver and the Gentle Reader." *Imagined Worlds: Essays on Some English Novels and Novelists in Honor of John Butt*. Ed. Maynard Mack and Ian Gregor. London: Methuen, 1968. 51-90.

————. *Gulliver and the Gentle Reader: Studies in Swift and Our Time*. Boston: Routledge, 1973.

Reichard, Hugo M. "Gulliver the Pretender." *Papers on English Language and Literature* 1 (1965): 316-26.

————. "Satiric Snobbery: The Houyhnhnms' Man." *Satire Newsletter* 4 (1967): 51-57.

Reichert, John F. "Plato, Swift, and the Houyhnhnms." *Philological Quarterly* 47 (1968): 179-92.

Richetti, John J. *Popular Fiction before Richardson: Narrative Patterns, 1700-1739*. Oxford: Clarendon, 1969.

Riely, John. "Scribleriana at the Yale Center for British Art." *Scriblerian* 10 (1977): 47-50.

Rodino, Richard H. *Swift Studies, 1965-1980: An Annotated Bibliography.* Garland Reference Library of the Humanities 386. New York: Garland, 1984.

Rosenheim, Edward, Jr. "The Fifth Voyage of Lemuel Gulliver." *Modern Philology* 60 (1962): 103-19.

———. *Swift and the Satirist's Art.* Chicago: U of Chicago P, 1963.

Ross, John F. "The Final Comedy of Lemuel Gulliver." *Studies in the Comic.* U of California Publications in English 8.2. Berkeley: U of California P, 1941. 175-96.

———. *Swift and Defoe: A Study in Relationship.* Berkeley: U of California P, 1941.

Rousseau, Jean-Jacques. *The Social Contract and Discourse on the Origin and Foundation of Inequality among Mankind.* 1762. Ed. Lester Crocker. New York: Pocket, 1971.

Rudat, Wolfgang E. H. "Pope's Clarissa, the Trojan Horse, and Swift's Houyhnhnms." *Forum for Modern Language Studies* 13 (1977): 6-11.

Sackett, S. J. "Gulliver Four: Here We Go Again." *Bulletin of the Rocky Mountain Modern Language Association* 27 (1973): 212-18.

Sacks, Sheldon. *Fiction and the Shape of Belief.* Berkeley: U of California P, 1967.

Said, Edward W. "Swift's Tory Anarchy." *Eighteenth-Century Studies* 3 (1969): 48-66.

"Der Satyr Silenus." *Catalogue of Prints and Drawings in the British Museum.* London, 1873. No. 1516.

Schine, Cathleen. "Seek Dwellings for MX." *New Yorker* 14 Feb. 1983: 41.

Sena, John. "The Language of Gestures in *Gulliver's Travels.*" *Papers on Language and Literature* 19 (1983): 145-66.

———. "Swift, the Yahoos, and 'The English Malady.'" *Papers on Language and Literature* 7 (1971): 300-03.

Shaftesbury, Anthony Ashley Cooper, 3rd Earl of. *Characteristics of Men, Manners, Opinion, Times.* Ed. John M. Robertson. 2 vols. London: Richards, 1900.

Shamsuddoha, M. "Swift's Moral Satire in the Fourth Book of *Gulliver's Travels.*" *Dacca University Studies* 23 (1975): A83-94.

Sherbo, Arthur. "Swift and Travel Literature." *Modern Language Studies* 9.3 (1979): 114-27.

Sherburn, George. "Errors Concerning the Houyhnhnms." *Modern Philology* 56 (1958): 92-97.

Sherwin, Judith Johnson. "The Voyages of a Mile-High *Fille de Joie.*" *Playboy* 24 Apr. 1977: 114+; noted in *Scriblerian* 8 (1978): 55.

Skinner, B. F. *Walden Two.* New York: Macmillan, 1962.

Smedley, Jonathan. *Gulliveriana: Or, A Fourth Volume of Miscellanies.* London, 1728; portions rpt. in *Gulliveriana VI.*

Smith, Raymond J., Jr. "The 'Character' of Lemuel Gulliver." *Tennessee Studies in Literature* 10 (1965): 133-39.

Soyinka, Wole. "Gulliver." *A Shuttle in the Crypt.* New York: Hill & Wang, 1972. Rpt. in *Scriblerian* 13 (1981): 128-29.

Sprat, Thomas. *The History of the Royal Society.* 1667. Ed. Jackson I. Cope and Harold Whitmore Jones. St. Louis: Washington UP, 1958.

Stathis, James J. *A Bibliography of Swift Studies, 1945-65.* Nashville: Vanderbilt UP, 1967.

Steele, Peter. "Terminal Days among the Houyhnhnms." *Southern Review* (Adelaide) 4 (1971): 227-36.

Stephens, F. G., and Mary Dorothy George, eds. *A Catalogue of Political and Personal Satires.* 1870-1954. 11 vols. in 12. London: British Museum, 1978.

Stone, Edward. "Swift and the Horses: Misanthropy or Comedy?" *Modern Language Quarterly* 10 (1949): 367-76.

Suits, Conrad. "The Role of the Horses in 'A Voyage to the Houyhnhnms.'" *University of Toronto Quarterly* 34 (1964-65): 118-32.

Suleiman, Susan R., and Inge Crosman, eds. *The Reader in the Text: Essays on Audience and Interpretation.* Princeton: Princeton UP, 1980.

Sutherland, John N. "A Reconsideration of Gulliver's Third Voyage." *Studies in Philology* 54 (1957): 45-52.

Swift, Jonathan. *The Annotated* Gulliver's Travels. Ed. Isaac Asimov. New York: Crown, 1980.

——. *The Correspondence of Jonathan Swift.* Ed. Harold Williams. 5 vols. Oxford: Clarendon, 1963-65.

——. *Gulliver's Travels.* London, 1865.

——. *Gulliver's Travels.* Paris, 1875.

——. *Gulliver's Travels.* London, 1894.

——. *Gulliver's Travels.* London: Dent; New York: Dutton, 1909.

——. *Gulliver's Travels.* Classics Illustrated 16. New York: Gilberton, 1946.

——. *Gulliver's Travels.* New York: Crown, 1947.

——. *Gulliver's Travels.* Ed. Louis A. Landa. Boston: Houghton, 1960.

——. *Gulliver's Travels.* New York: NAL, 1960

——. *Gulliver's Travels.* Ed. Robert A. Greenberg. New York: Norton, 1970.

——. *Gulliver's Travels.* Arlington: Great Ocean, 1980.

——. *Gulliver's Travels.* Forward by Marcus Cunliffe. New York: Signet, 1980.

——. *Gulliver's Travels* (selections). *The Norton Anthology of English Literature.* Ed. M. H. Abrams et al. 4th ed. 2 vols. New York: Norton, 1979. 1: 1970-2144.

——. *Gulliver's Travels* (selections). *The Norton Anthology of English Literature: Major Authors Edition.* Ed. M. H. Abrams et al. 3rd ed. New York: Norton, 1975. 941-1113.

——. *Gulliver's Travels* (selections). *The Norton Anthology of World Masterpieces.* Ed. Maynard Mack et al. 4th ed. 2 vols. New York: Norton, 1979. 1: 165-224.

——. *Gulliver's Travels* (selections). *The Restoration and the Eighteenth Century.* Ed. Martin Price. Oxford Anthology of English Literature Series. New York: Oxford UP, 1973. 236-90.

——. Gulliver's Travels: *The Text of the First Edition.* Ed. Harold Williams. London: Clowes, 1927.

——. Gulliver's Travels *and Other Writings.* Ed. Ricardo Quintana. New York: Modern Library, 1958.

——. Gulliver's Travels *and Other Writings.* Ed. Louis A. Landa. Boston: Houghton Mifflin, 1960.

——. *Jonathan Swift.* Ed. Angus Ross and David Woolley. Oxford Authors Series. New York: Oxford UP, 1984.

——. *Letters of Jonathan Swift to Charles Ford.* Ed. David Nichol Smith. Oxford: Clarendon, 1935.

——. *The Poems of Jonathan Swift.* Ed. Harold Williams. 2nd ed. 3 vols. Oxford: Clarendon, 1958.

——. *The Prose Works of Jonathan Swift.* Ed. Herbert J. Davis et al. 14 vols. Oxford: Blackwell, 1939-68.

——. *Swift:* Gulliver's Travels *and Other Writings.* Ed. Miriam Kosh Starkman. New York: Bantam, 1965.

——. *A Tale of a Tub.* Ed. A. C. Guthkelch and David Nichol Smith. 2nd ed. Oxford: Clarendon, 1958.

——. *Voyages de Gulliver.* Paris, 1797.

——. *The Works of the Reverend Dr. Jonathan Swift.* Ed. George Faulkner. 11 vols. Dublin, 1762.

——. *The Writings of Jonathan Swift.* Ed. Robert A. Greenberg and William B. Piper. New York: Norton, 1973.

Swift, Jonathan, et al. *Memoirs of the Extraordinary Life, Works, and Discoveries of Martinus Scriblerus.* Ed. Charles Kerby-Miller. New Haven: Yale UP, 1950.

Takase, Fumiko. "The Houyhnhnms and the Eighteenth-Century Goût Chinois." *English Studies* 61 (1980): 408-17.

Taylor, Aline M. "Cyrano de Bergerac and Gulliver's 'Voyage to Brobding-nag.'" *Tulane Studies in English* 5 (1955): 83-102.

——. "Sights and Monsters and Gulliver's Voyage to Brobdingnag." *Tulane Studies in English* 7 (1957): 28-82.

Teerink, Hermann. *A Bibliography of the Writings of Jonathan Swift.* Rev. H. Teerink. Ed. Arthur Scouten. 2nd ed. Philadelphia: U of Pennsylvania P, 1963.

Telemann, Georg. *Gulliver-Suite*. In *Hortus Musicus*. Barenreiter: Kassell and Basel, 1949. Vol. 11.

Temple, Sir William. *The Letters of Sir W. Temple*. 2 vols. London, 1700.

Terenzi, Hector, and Jose Reissig. *Genetics* 56 (1967): 321.

Thomas, W. K. "Satiric Catharsis." *University of Windsor Review* 3.2 (1968): 33-44.

Thorpe, Peter. "The Economics of Satire: Towards a New Definition." *Western Humanities Review* 23 (1969): 187-96.

Tobin, James E., and Louis A. Landa. *Jonathan Swift: A List of Critical Studies Published from 1895-1945*. New York: Cosmopolitan Science and Art, 1945.

Tompkins, Jane P., ed. *Reader-Response Criticism: From Formalism to Post-Structuralism*. Baltimore: Johns Hopkins UP, 1980.

Torchiana, Donald T. "Jonathan Swift, the Irish, and the Yahoos: The Case Reconsidered." *Philological Quarterly* 54 (1975): 195-212.

Tracy, Clarence. "The Unity of *Gulliver's Travels*." *Queen's Quarterly* 68 (1962): 597-609.

Traldi, Ila Dawson. "Gulliver the 'Educated Fool': Unity in the Voyage to Laputa." *Papers on Language and Literature* 4 (1968): 35-50.

Traugott, John, ed. *Discussions of Jonathan Swift*. Boston: Heath, 1962.

――――. "A Voyage to Nowhere with Thomas More and Jonathan Swift: *Utopia* and *The Voyage to the Houyhnhnms*." *Sewanee Review* 69 (1961): 534-65.

Trimmer, Joseph F. "A Note on Gulliver and the Four Captains." *Ball State University Forum* 12.2 (1971): 39-43.

Tuveson, Ernest, ed. *Swift: A Collection of Critical Essays*. Twentieth-Century Views. Englewood Cliffs: Prentice, 1964.

――――. "Swift: The Dean as Satirist." *University of Toronto Quarterly* 22 (1953): 308-75.

Uphaus, Robert W. *The Impossible Observer: Reason and the Reader in Eighteenth-Century Prose*. Lexington: UP of Kentucky, 1979.

Vance, John A. " 'The Odious Vermin': Gulliver's Progression towards Misanthropy." *Enlightenment Essays* 10 (1979): 65-73.

Van Loen, Alfred. *Drawings*. New York: Harbor Gallery, 1969.

Vickers, Brian. "The Satiric Structure of *Gulliver's Travels* and More's *Utopia*." *The World of Jonathan Swift*. Ed. Vickers. Cambridge: Harvard UP; Oxford: Blackwell, 1968. 233-57.

Vieth, D. M. *Swift's Poetry, 1900-1980: An Annotated Bibliography*. New York: Garland, 1982.

Voigt, Milton. *Swift and the Twentieth Century*. Detroit: Wayne State UP, 1968.

Voltaire. *Candide*. 1759. Trans. and ed. Robert M. Adams. New York: Norton, 1966.

Walpole, Horace. "The Sequel to *Gulliver's Travels.*" In Walpole to the Countess of Upper Ossory, 14 Dec. 1771. *The Yale Edition of Horace Walpole's Correspondence.* Ed. W. S. Lewis, A. G. Wallace, and E. M. Martz. New Haven: Yale UP, 1965. 32: 71-73.

Watkins, W. B. C. *Perilous Balance.* Princeton: Princeton UP, 1939.

Watt, Ian. *Conrad in the Nineteenth Century.* Berkeley: U of California Press, 1979.

Wedel, T. O. "On the Philosophical Background of *Gulliver's Travels.*" *Studies in Philology* 23 (1926): 434-50.

Welcher, J. K. "Gulliver in the Market-Place." *Studies on Voltaire and the Eighteenth Century* 217 (1983): 125-39.

———. "Horace Walpole and *Gulliver's Travels.*" *Studies in Eighteenth-Century Culture* 12 (1983): 45-57.

———. "Swift-Hogarth Give and Take." *Ventures in Research, Long Island University* 3 (1974): 23-52.

Welcher, Jeanne K., and Randi Joseph. "Gulliverian Drawings by Richard Wilson." *Eighteenth-Century Studies* 18 (1985): 170-85.

White, Douglas H. "Swift and the Definition of Man." *Modern Philology* 73 (1976): S48-S55.

White, John H. "Swift's Trojan Horses: 'Reasoning But to Err.'" *English Language Notes* 3 (1966): 185-94.

Wilding, Michael. "The Politics of *Gulliver's Travels.*" *Studies in the Eighteenth Century.* Vol. 2. Ed. R. F. Brissenden. Canberra: Australian National UP; Toronto: U of Toronto P, 1973. 303-22.

Wilkins, John. *Mathematicall Magick: Or, The Wonders That May Be Perform'd by Mechanical Geometry.* London, 1648.

Willey, Basil. *The Eighteenth Century Background.* London: Chatto, 1940.

Williams, Kathleen. "Gulliver's Voyage to the Houyhnhnms." *Journal of English Literary History* 18 (1951): 275-86.

———. *Jonathan Swift and the Age of Compromise.* Lawrence: U of Kansas P, 1958.

———, ed. *Swift: The Critical Heritage.* London: Routledge; New York: Barnes, 1970.

Wilson, James R. "Swift, the Psalmist, and the Horse." *Tennessee Studies in Literature* 3 (1958): 17-23.

Wimsatt, William K. *Philosophic Words: A Study of the Style and Meaning in the Rambler and Dictionary of Samuel Johnson.* New Haven: Yale UP, 1948.

Winton, Calhoun. "Conversion on the Road to Houyhnhnmland." *Sewanee Review* 68 (1960): 20-33.

Yeomans, W. E. "The Houyhnhnm as Menippean Horse." *College English* 27 (1966): 449-54.

Zimansky, Curt A. "Gulliver, Yahoos, and Critics." *College English* 27 (1965): 45-49.

Zimmerman, Everett. "Gulliver the Preacher." *PMLA* 89 (1974): 1024-32.

———. *Swift's Narrative Satires: Author and Authority*. Ithaca: Cornell UP, 1983.

Zirker, Herbert. "Lemuel Gullivers *Yahoos* und Swifts Satire." *Anglia* 87 (1969): 39-63.

Index

Adams, Percy G., 84
Addams, Charles, 96
Aikins, Janet E., 16, 37
Akutagawa, 96
Alexander the Great, 59
Allison, Alexander W., 24
The Anatomist Dissected, 100
Anne, Queen, 25
Ansell, C., 101
Arbuthnot, John, 57, 86, 98, 103
Argyle, Michael, 49
Aristotle, 59, 61, 82
Ashley, Maurice, 10
Asimov, Isaac, 7
Augustine, Saint, 102
Augustus, 59

Bantley, R. (pseud.), 99
Beauchamp, Gorman, 19, 24
Beckett, J. C., 10
Bellamy, Edward, 117
Bentley, Richard, 82
Bentman, Raymond, 24
Bergerac, Savinien de Cyrano de, 102
Bergson, Henri, 44
Bleywick, F., 101
A Blunder of All Blunders: Or, Gulliver Devour'd by Butterflies, 100
Bolingbroke, Henry St. John, first viscount, 46, 82, 94, 98–99, 102
Bolingbroke, Lady (Marquise de Villette), 98
Bonner, William Hallam, 86
Bony, Alain, 24, 37
Booth, Wayne C., 18
Boswell, James, 30, 56, 78
Bowen, Mary Elizabeth, 7
Boyce, Benjamin, 82
Boyle, John, fifth earl of Orrery, 63
Bracher, Frederick, 86
Brady, Frank, 12, 22, 37, 84
Brengle, Richard L., 97
Brink, J. R., 19
Brock, C. E., 49, 50–51
Brooks, Mel, 118
Brown, Norman, 12
Brutus, Marcus Junius, 59
Bulfinch, Thomas, 117
Bullitt, John, 11

Caesar, Gaius Julius, 59

Carnochan, W. B., 11, 24, 37
Caroline of Anspach (wife of George II), 98
Case, Arthur, 11, 86
Castle, Terry J., 19, 24
Cervantes, Miguel de, 102
Chaplin, Charles, 44
Churchill, Sarah, Duchess of Marlborough, 82
Cibber, Colley, 99
Clifford, James L., 12, 15, 18–19, 20, 21–22, 24, 48, 120
Clubb, Merrell D., 22
Cohan, Steven M., 24
Coleridge, Samuel Taylor, 57
Cook, Terry, 24
Corman, Brian, 16, 63
Crane, R. S., 6, 11, 12, 19, 22, 34, 37, 64
Crosman, Inge, 25
Cruikshank, Isaac, 98, 101
Culler, Jonathan, 25
Cunliffe, Marcus, 4
Curll, Edmund, 100

Daggett, David, 100
Dampier, William, 6, 84–86, 102
Davis, Herbert J., 9, 15, 26, 30, 39, 58, 63, 69, 82, 92, 100
Defoe, Daniel, 6, 83, 84, 122
Dennis, Nigel, 83
Deon, Michel, 96
DePorte, Michael, 5, 16, 57
De Quincey, Thomas, 63
Descartes, René, 59, 102
Desfontaines, Abbé, 102, 103
Dickens, Charles, 45
Dickinson, Emily, 26
Diderot, Denis, 98
Dobrée, Bonamy, 61
Donne, John, 90
Donoghue, Denis, 22, 63
Dryden, John, 66
Duthie, Elizabeth, 101
Dyson, A. E., 24

Easthope, A. K., 24
Eddy, William A., 57, 81, 97
Ehrenpreis, Irvin, 6, 11, 19, 22, 38, 64–65, 81, 88
"The English Rope-Dancer," 107–108

Erasmus, Desiderius, 102
Escher, M. C., 120

Fagnan, Marie Antoinette, 101
Faulkner, George, 3, 38
Fénelon, François de Salignac de La Mothe, 102
Ferguson, Oliver, 10
Fetrow, Fred M., 24
Fielding, Henry, 98, 100, 103, 107
Fish, Stanley, 25
Fitzgerald, Robert P., 24
Fludd, Robert, 105–06
Foigny, Gabriel de, 83
Ford, Charles, 97, 98
Foster, Milton P., 12, 22
Fox, Christopher, 16, 69
Franklin, Benjamin, 98
Frantz, R. W., 86
Frazer, James George, 117–18
Freud, Sigmund, 44
Frye, Roland, 12, 48
Fussell, Paul, 10, 46

Garrick, David, 100
Gassendi, Pierre, 59
Gay, John, 57, 81, 98, 122
Gelli (Aulus Gellius), 102
George, Dorothy, 10, 97, 100, 101
George I, 102
Gilbert, William, 87
Gill, James E., 19, 23, 24
Gillray, James, 101
Gilpin, Sawrey, 101
Goldgar, Bertrand, 10
Goldin, Frederick, 73
Gosse, Edmund, 64
Gottlieb, Sidney, 16, 52
Goulding, Sybil, 97
Gove, Philip Babcock, 97
Goya, Francisco de, 101
Grandville, Jean Ignace Isidore Gerard, 49, 50, 51
Gravil, Richard, 22
Greenberg, Robert A., 3, 89
Greene, Donald, 10, 19, 22, 24
Guinness, Alec, 109
Gulliveriana, 97–98
Guthkelch, A. C., 105

Hakluyt, Richard, 104
Halewood, William H., 19, 23
Harley, Robert, first earl of Oxford, 46, 82, 102
Harris, James, 63
Harris, Richard, 7
Harth, Phillip, 11, 40

Hassall, Anthony J., 24
Hawkesworth, John, 64
Haywood, Eliza, 98
Hobbes, Thomas, 44, 102
Hodgart, Matthew, 96
Hogarth, William, 76, 100–01, 104
Holberg, Ludvig, 98, 99
Holly, Grant, 24, 100
Holmes, Geoffrey Shorter, 10
Homer, 61, 82
Hooke, Robert, 102, 104–105
Horace (Quintus Horatius Flaccus), 22, 23
Housman, A. E., 126
Howells, William Dean, 117
Hutcheson, Francis, 83
Huxley, Aldous, 117–18, 120

Ile de la Folie, 99
Ingarden, Roman, 25
Iser, Wolfgang, 25, 28, 29
It Cannot Rain but It Pours, 99

James II, 107
Jeffares, A. Norman, 12, 88
Jeffrey, Francis, 57
Johnson, J. W., 117–18
Johnson, Samuel, 30, 56, 78, 91, 100
Jones, Richard Foster, 10
Joseph, Randi, 101
Juvenal (Decimus Junius Juvenalis), 119

Kallich, Martin, 19, 22
Karinthy, Frigyes, 96
Karl, Frederick R., 83
Keener, Frederick M., 82
Keesey, Donald, 23
Kelling, H. D., 22, 24
Kelly, Ann Cline, 19, 23
Kelsall, M. M., 22, 23
Kenner, Hugh, 81
Kenyon, J. P., 10
Kinsley, William, 37
Knowles, A. S., Jr., 23
Korshin, Paul, 87
Kramnick, Isaac, 10

LaCasce, Steward, 23, 24
La Fontaine, Jean de, 73–74
Lalauze, A. D., 49, 51
Landa, Louis, 3, 9, 11, 19, 23, 24, 46, 75, 89
La Rochefoucauld, François, sixth duc de, 102
Leavis, F. R., 64

LeFebvre, 49, 50, 51, 98, 101
Leibniz, Gottfried, Wilhelm von, 83
Leigh, David J., 8, 16, 109
Leigh, Jon S., 19
Lenfest, David S., 51, 97, 98, 101
Levich, Marvin, 19, 23
Leyburn, Ellen Douglass, 86
Un lezione su d'un vitello a due teste delle Accademico delle Scienze colle note di Lemuel Gulliver, 100
Lind, Jakov, 96
A Little More of That Same, 96
Lock, F. P., 11, 40
Locke, John, 102
Louis XIV, 108
Lovejoy, Arthur, 11
Lucian, 102
Lund, Roger D., 16, 81

Mack, Maynard, 83
"The Majestic Clockwork," 7
Malraux, André, 101
Mandeville, Bernard, 72
Manley, Delarivière, 82
Manley, Mary, 83
Marivaux, Pierre Carlet de Chamblain de, 98
McDermot, Murtagh (pseud.), 99
McManmon, John J., 19, 23
Memoirs of the Court of Lilliput, 99
Merton, Robert C., 87
Meyers, Jeffrey, 120
Mezciems, Jenny, 57
Mill, John Stuart, 117, 120
Miller, Robert Keith, 17, 123
Milton, John, 56
Mist, Nathaniel, 99
Modern Gulliver's Travels, 100
Moffett, James, 126, 128
Mohler, Nora, 10, 48, 57, 87, 88
Moll, Herman, 86
Monk, Samuel Holt, 6, 12
Montaigne, Michel Eyquem de, 102, 118
Montesquieu, Charles Louis de Secondat, Baron de la Brède et de, 6
Moore, Cecil A., 49
Moore, John B., 24
Moore, Sir Jonas, 105–06
More, Thomas, 19, 59, 102, 117
Morley, Henry, 107–08
Morris, Desmond, 49
Morris, John, 23
Morten, Thomas, 49, 50, 51
Munro, John, 57
Murray, Douglas, 17, 121, 126

Nicolson, Marjorie, 10, 48, 57, 87, 88
Nokes, David, 11
Nordon, Pierre, 24
Novak, Maximilian E., 19

Oakleaf, David, 37
Onania: Or, The Heinous Sin of Self-Pollution, and All Its Frightful Consequences, 72
Orwell, George, 117–18, 120
Otten, Robert M., 24
Ovid (Publius Ovidius Naso), 72–73

Palomo, Dolores, 16, 75
Peake, Charles, 22
Pendarves, Mary, 94–95
Peter the Wild Boy, 99
Phillipson, John S., 23–24
Philmus, Robert M., 19, 23, 24
Philosophical Transactions of the Royal Society of London, 6, 48, 87, 88, 122
Pierre, Gerald J., 19, 23
Piper, William B., 3, 89
Plato, 22, 23, 102, 117, 119
Plumb, J. H., 10
Plutarch, 19, 22, 23
Pope, Alexander, 3, 20, 25, 34, 49, 64, 65, 81, 82, 98, 127
Porter, Roy, 10
Price, Martin, 5
Probyn, Clive T., 11, 12, 19, 37
Pullen, Charles H., 16, 24, 89
Pyle, Fitzroy, 23

Quinlan, Maurice J., 82
Quintana, Ricardo, 4, 6, 11, 19, 24, 57, 61, 86
Quintanilla, Luis, 49, 51

Rabb, Melinda Alliker, 7, 16, 102
Rabelais, Francois, 102
Rabkin, Eric, 50
Rackham, Arthur, 49, 51
Rader, Ralph W., 66–67
Radner, John B., 19, 23
Raspe, Rudolf, 98
Rawson, C. J., 11, 12, 24, 64, 65
Reaves, R B, 16, 113
Redgrave, Michael, 7
Reichard, Hugo M., 23, 24
Reichert, John F., 19, 23
Reissig, Jose, 96–97
Richardson, Katherine, 90–93
Richetti, John J., 82, 84
Rielly, Edward J., 1, 17, 121

Riely, John, 101
Rodino, Richard H., 10, 12, 15, 18, 24
Rooke, George, 108
Rosenheim, Edward, Jr., 11, 22, 39, 67
Ross, Angus, 7, 9
Ross, John F., 22, 23, 83
Rousseau, Jean-Jacques, 117, 118
Rudat, Wolfgang, 24

Sackett, S. J., 24
Sacks, Sheldon, 41
Said, Edward W., 81
"Der Satyr Silenus," 105, 106–107
Schakel, Peter J., 16, 30
Schine, Cathleen, 126
Scott, Walter, 84
Sena, John F., 7, 16, 44
Shaftesbury, Anthony Ashley Cooper, third earl of, 83
Shakespeare, William, 126
Shamsuddoha, M., 22
Sherbo, Arthur, 84
Sherburn, George, 18, 22
Sherwin, Judith Johnson, 96
Skinner, B. F., 117, 120
Smedley, Jonathan, 98
Smith, David Nichol, 105
Smith, Frederik N., 15, 25, 121
Smith, Raymond J., Jr., 24
Smollett, Tobias, 77
Soyinka, Wole, 96
Sprat, Thomas, 86, 88, 102
Starkman, Miriam Kosh, 4
Stathis, James J., 10, 24
Steele, Peter, 24
Stella (Esther Johnson), 98
Stephens, F. G., 97, 100, 101
Stone, Edward, 37
Suits, Conrad, 22, 24, 37
Suleiman, Susan R., 25
Sutherland, John N., 57
Symson, William, 84

Takase, Fumiko, 19, 23
Taylor, Aline M., 11, 81
Teerink, Hermann, 10, 97
Telemann, Georg, 7, 49
Temple, William, 22, 23
Terenzi, Hector, 97
Thackeray, William Makepeace, 63
Thomas, W. K., 23
Thorpe, Peter, 19, 23
Tobin, James E., 9, 24
Tofts, Mary, 100

Tompkins, Jane P., 25
Torchiana, Donald T., 19
Tracy, Clarence, 22
Traldi, Ila Dawson, 56
Traugott, John, 12, 19, 24, 81
Travels into Several Remote Nations, 100
Trimmer, Joseph F., 24
Tuveson, Ernest, 12, 22

Uphaus, Robert W., 37, 43

Vance, John A., 24
Van Loen, Alfred, 96
Veiras, Denis, 83
Vickers, Brian, 19
Vieth, D. M., 10
Voigt, Milton, 10, 16–17, 22, 81, 117
Voltaire (François Marie Arouet), 6, 98, 99, 103
Voyage to Cacklogallinia, 99
"Vygos Cagados," 108

Walpole, Horace, 98, 101
Walpole, Robert, 40, 102, 107
Ward, Edward, 102
Watkins, W. B. C., 22
Watt, Ian, 54
Wedel, T. O., 19, 83
Welcher, Jeanne K., 7, 16, 96, 98, 100, 101
Wesley, John, 64
White, Douglas H., 19
White, John H., 19, 23
White, T. H., 96
Wilding, Michael, 19, 23
Wilkins, John, 105
Willey, Basil, 10
Williams, Harold, 9, 89, 95
Williams, Kathleen, 11, 12, 22, 23, 56, 63, 83, 84, 102–03
Wilson, James R., 22
Wilson, Richard, 101
Wimsatt, William K., 87
Winton, Calhoun, 22
Woodward, George, 101
Woolley, David, 9

Yeomans, W. E., 19, 23

Zimansky, Curt A., 23
Zimmerman, Everett, 24
Zinker, Herbert, 23